Horary Astrology

Step by Step

Also by Petros Eleftheriadis

Horary Astrology:
The Practical Way to Learn your Fate

Horary Astrology

Step by Step

Petros Eleftheriadis

The Wessex Astrologer

Published in 2021 by
The Wessex Astrologer Ltd
PO Box 9307
Swanage
BH19 9BF

For a full list of our titles go to www.wessexastrologer.com

© Petros Eleftheriadis 2021
Petros Eleftheriadis asserts his moral right to be recognised as
the author of this work

Cover design by Jonathan Taylor

A catalogue record for this book is available at The British Library

ISBN 9781910531532

No part of this book may be reproduced or used in any form or by any
means without the written permission of the publisher.
A reviewer may quote brief passages.

Contents

Introduction	vii
Part One Chart Validity	1
Part Two Casting the Chart/Finding Significators	9
Part Three Assessing the Significators	23
Part Four The Final Step – Chart Judgement	55
Appendix Extra Charts for Further Practice	85
The QHP Horary Course	99

Introduction

IN MY FIRST BOOK, *Horary Astrology, the Practical Way to Learn Your Fate*, I felt the need to write a book that included radical charts, because the only thing that I seemed to see everywhere, be it internet forums or even books, was non-radical charts, that is, either invalid questions or charts which don't follow the basic considerations before judgement. So I made up a book of 55 radical charts with questions that can be answered with a YES or a NO and showed how traditional concepts and theory are enough to come to a conclusion and that it's not inadequate, as people who create their own methods seem to think.

As a teacher however, I realized that there is another obstacle. It seems that knowing your theory is not enough. A lot of people apparently have difficulty implementing the theory they've learned to actual charts. They present all their testimonies correctly, but they just can't decide on the outcome. Is essential dignity stronger than accidental debility or is it the other way round? Which testimonies are more important than others? Is it possible to put an order to this chaos? Yes. This is what I will attempt to do in this book.

This book is a step by step guide to handling a horary chart. All the basic elements of theory are going to be presented, but the focus will be on the things that you absolutely need to know and understand. This is not going to be a book that will drown you in details about how Bonatti said this and Lilly said that. I always aim for practicality and my goal ever since the beginning of my astrology studies was to become a good astrology practitioner, not an astrology scholar. All the books and all the knowledge are out there, but if you can't make a distinction between what actually works and what doesn't, then all this knowledge goes to waste.

Have there been any changes since my first book? Not many. It's just that I have become stricter. As time goes by and I see people around me casting horary charts for practically no reason at all, I become more and more of a staunch supporter of the limited use of horary. As far as my theory goes, I have upgraded the Moon to the most important planetary body in horary astrology. I now consider the Moon to be void of course not only when she makes no aspects before she leaves the sign she is in, but even when her next aspect is more than 12 – 15 degrees away or thereabouts, depending on her daily speed. Finally, I believe that the Moon's conjunction with the South Node is a very negative testimony, much more than I thought in the past.

For all the rest, just dive in. Read and enjoy!

STEP ONE

CHART VALIDITY

Before we talk about chart validity, let's make one thing clear: The chart is cast using the place of the astrologer and the time the astrologer understands the question. A horary chart is like a birth chart in many ways. Just like we don't use conception charts for babies in nativity work, we don't use in horary charts the time the querent first came up with a question. The astrologer plays the role of the obstetrician in horary astrology and he or she is the one who "delivers" the question. Now, let's move on to chart validity.

Is our chart valid? This may seem simple, but it isn't. Contrary to how horary is being used currently, astrology is not an art or a science or whatever you want to call it, that tells you what to do. Astrology can't be used to offer us advice. The only thing astrology can do is tell us what is going to happen. Nothing else. So if your question is in any way trying to change the future or you are at a crossroads and you want astrology to tell you what's best for you to do, the chart you will cast is invalid. Astrology is not a tool that can make our life easier. Knowing the future doesn't mean altering the future. So:

a) Any question that begins with "Should I?" is invalid. Astrology cannot make your choices for you.

b) Questions like: 'Will I win if I play the lottery?", "Which job is best, job A or job B? This is another form of a "Should I" question. Invalid. Let me say this once more, astrology cannot tell you what to do, it can only tell you what will happen. We do not have a crystal ball and therefore we cannot always be very precise regarding what exactly is going to happen, but this is the best that we can do and we do not have any powers of intervention.

c) Third party questions: Unless the question is about a child, parent, husband/wife, sister/brother or perhaps a very close friend, the questions about the rest of the people you know are almost always asked out of curiosity. Curiosity is not a reason to cast a horary chart. Also, questions like: "Is John seeing another woman/man?" This is a question asked out of curiosity and rather pointless, to be honest. The real question here is: "Is my relationship going well/threatened?", "Are we breaking up/getting divorced?" If the chart shows another person involved, fine, but don't make the question about them.

d) Ask questions that are answered with a YES or a NO. Don't ask questions like: "Who called me last night?" Let's say that the chart says that it's a 3rd house person. Is it a brother, a sister, a neighbour or a friend's child (5th from the 11th)? One can never know for sure, so the question is usually pointless. Also, avoid vague questions like: "What exactly does he want from me?" Horary is a method designed to provide simple answers to straightforward questions. Don't make things complicated.

e) Don't ask questions that beat about the bush: "Will I go out with John this Saturday?" or "Am I in his thoughts?" What do you want to know that for? If John is someone you are interested in, then the real question is "Will we be together?" That's all you need to know. Usually, when people ask this kind of question, something is not going well and instead of asking the important thing, they ask all sorts of questions around the issue, because they would rather not face the truth. Or they got a negative answer in the past and now they are asking something different hoping for something positive this time round.

f) Try not to ask questions about politics or mundane events in general: Horary astrology is not the best astrological method for this. You can ask about a candidate or a party you strongly support whether they will win or not, but try to avoid an impartial "Who will win?" question, although

I must admit, I have asked similar questions in the past, but now I've decided to practise what I preach. I'm more of the opinion now that the chart needs to be as personal as possible. Instead, for "Who will win?" questions, use the charts for ingresses and solstices or nativities for politicians, if there is an accurate birth time.

g) Don't ask questions with a time frame. It's pointless, and usually makes the question invalid. Questions like: "Will I get a job in the next six months?" are invalid. What if you get a job in seven months? The chart must say no, but it usually doesn't. If you are indeed looking for a job, then simply ask: "Will I get a job?" and leave the time frame out of this. Don't fool yourself into believing that you can phrase the question the way you want it and that this makes a difference to the universe. No, the universe knows what you are really asking behind your silly phrasing, so just ask it. This is usually a trick used by astrologers so that their clients don't get disappointed. "You are not going to get a job in the next six months, but who knows what will happen in seven months?" Horary astrology has a limited time frame by definition and usually deals with procedures that have already begun in real time. We don't move the planets beyond the sign they are in, unless they are about to change signs, so just because the answer is negative to a "Will I get a job?" question, this doesn't mean that the querent will never get a job in their lifetime. It just means that they won't get a job in the immediate future. Anyway, the best way to handle this is to ask a question about a job you've already applied for.

h) Don't ask questions that have no connection with the present. Questions like: "Will I ever have a relationship again?" asked at a moment when there is no love interest in sight or: "Will I ever have a baby?" asked at a time when the querent is not making attempts to have a baby, are invalid. These questions are best suited for nativities. As I have already said, horary charts are cast for events likely to happen in the near future and have somehow begun to unravel (one is looking for a job, one is trying to have a baby, one has met a significant other etc.)

i) Don't ask questions that are too specific even for horary astrology. For example: "I feel sick, do I have the coronavirus?". The chart will tell you if you are sick and when or if you'll get better, it cannot make such a precise diagnosis. The fact that you ask about coronavirus doesn't mean that the chart is going to show you in perfect health if you don't have it. If you are sick, the chart is going to show this whether it's the coronavirus or just plain flu.

Note: It's always good when the ascending sign of the horary chart is the same as the ascending sign of the querent. The Moon or the ruler of the ascendant in the house of the quesited is also a good sign and these things help to establish radicality.

Now, after the question has passed all of the above criteria, we need to check the considerations before judgement. These are some prerequisites established by astrologers of the classical era, because they noticed that charts do not 'behave' well sometimes. The most important consideration for me is the void of course Moon. The Moon is by far the most important planetary body in a horary chart, even more important than the ascendant ruler, so we want her to be able to perform. The typical definition of a void of course Moon is when she makes no applying aspects to other planets until the moment she exits the sign she is in. However, if the Moon is at 29° degrees in a certain sign, has just separated from a planet at 27° degrees somewhere in the chart and she is about to make an aspect very soon after she changes sign, then we can't actually call her void. I consider the Moon void, though, when she does make an applying aspect before she exits the sign she is in, but that aspect is out of orb. Personally, if the Moon needs to travel more than 12 – 15 degrees to make an aspect, I find this Moon very problematic and even though in my first book, *Horary Astrology, the Practical Way to Learn*

Your Fate, I included a couple of charts with such a Moon, I would now probably put the chart aside. It all depends on the speed of the Moon. If the Moon needs more than a day (24 hours) for her next aspect, then I consider her void. This may be 15 degrees if the Moon is fast, or a little less than 12 degrees if the Moon is slow. Finally, I don't pay any attention to the Moon's sign, regarding her being void, that is. If one follows Lilly, he believed the void Moon to be able to perform when she is in Taurus, Cancer, Sagittarius, Pisces. I am not of the same opinion. I need the Moon to make an applying aspect within orb, regardless of her sign.

The next consideration in line is the combust ascendant ruler. Unless the question is about health or the combustion can be explained adequately in some other way, then this often shows that the querent is hiding something from the astrologer, is asking the wrong question or is unaware of certain facts that make the question invalid.

One other important consideration is when Mars or Saturn are in the 7th house, unless the question is about a 7th house matter. This does show sometimes that the astrologer will give a wrong answer. If you are asking your own questions, then you are your own astrologer, so this is not valid for you because you belong to the 1st house.

You should also make a note when there are early (0°00′ to 2°59′) or late (27°00′ to 29°59′) degrees of a sign ascending. This is perhaps the weakest consideration of all, because it doesn't make much sense. However, I must admit I feel uneasy when this comes up in a chart. As a general rule, I strongly advise you to cast the chart aside when two or three of the above considerations are present, for example, early degrees ascending, void of course Moon and combust ascendant ruler. This chart is not fit to be judged.

Finally, when a chart is considered invalid, there is a reason for this. The querent cannot just call the astrologer the next day for a new chart. From my experience, this seemingly valid chart of the next day can rarely produce an accurate result. There has to be a significant change in the matter propounded, something new that would urge the querent to ask again, quite possibly with an improved clarity of mind.

Step Two

Casting the Chart/ Finding the Significators

Which house system should we use? Most horary astrologers use the Regiomontanus house system, because it's the one William Lilly, the great astrologer of the Renaissance, used. I prefer Alcabitius or Porphyry, because these house systems divide the houses more equally. Can I make an assertion that Alcabitius is better than Regiomontanus? No. The moment I get too confident with Alcabitius (especially in natal work), a chart tends to come up that works better with Regiomontanus.

Now, where are the planets located? In which house, I mean. This is not as simple as it sounds. The problem with houses is that their meanings were established with the whole sign house system and now horary astrologers don't use that any more. For example, the 5th house is fortunate, because it's succedent (not cadent) and it trines the ascending sign in a chart cast using the whole sign house system. Using unequal house systems, though, the 5th house sign and planets therein do not necessarily trine the ascending sign and the question that arises is: Is that equally fortunate? I don't think so.

First of all, let's define angular planets. I consider a planet to be angular when it's in the SAME sign as the angle. So if the angle is at 29° Gemini, all planets in Gemini are considered to be angular. For planets that are very far from the angle, but in the same sign, you may find it difficult to call them angular, but I suggest you take into account that they are in the same sign and that boosts them a bit. For example, an MC at 29° Gemini, makes the sign of Gemini angular. If there is a planet at 1° Gemini, this is very far from the angle. You may keep it in the 9th house if you like, but you must treat it differently from another planet in the 9th house in the sign of Taurus. The planet in Taurus is a 9th house cadent planet, but the planet at 1° Gemini is a 9th house angular planet, therefore stronger.

In Example Chart 1, calculated using the Alcabitius system, the ascendant is in Aquarius and so is Saturn, on the 12th house side. You

12   Horary Astrology Step by Step

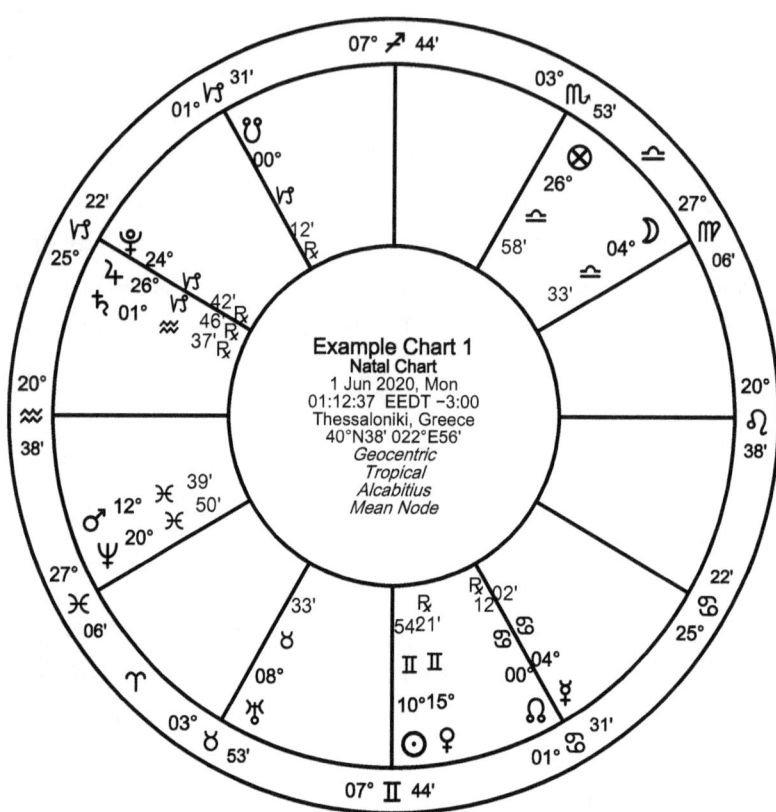

can either treat Saturn as a 1st house planet or, because he is quite far from the angle, as a 12th house planet, but you must make a distinction between Saturn and Jupiter. Both are in the 12th house, but Saturn beholds the ascendant and for him being in the 12th house is not so bad as it is for Jupiter. Mars may technically be in the 1st house, but he is in a different sign from the one in the ascendant, so he is not a 1st house planet. If this were a horary chart, Mars could not signify the querent.

If a planet is very close to an angle, but in a different sign from the angle, it cannot be called angular. For example, a planet at 1° Cancer in a chart with the MC at 29° Gemini is not angular. Can it be a 10th house planet, though not angular? Yes, if the whole sign of Cancer is intercepted in the 10th house or the chart has a Libra ascendant, which makes Cancer the natural 10th house sign. See Example Chart 2:

Step Two – Casting the Chart/Finding the Significators   13

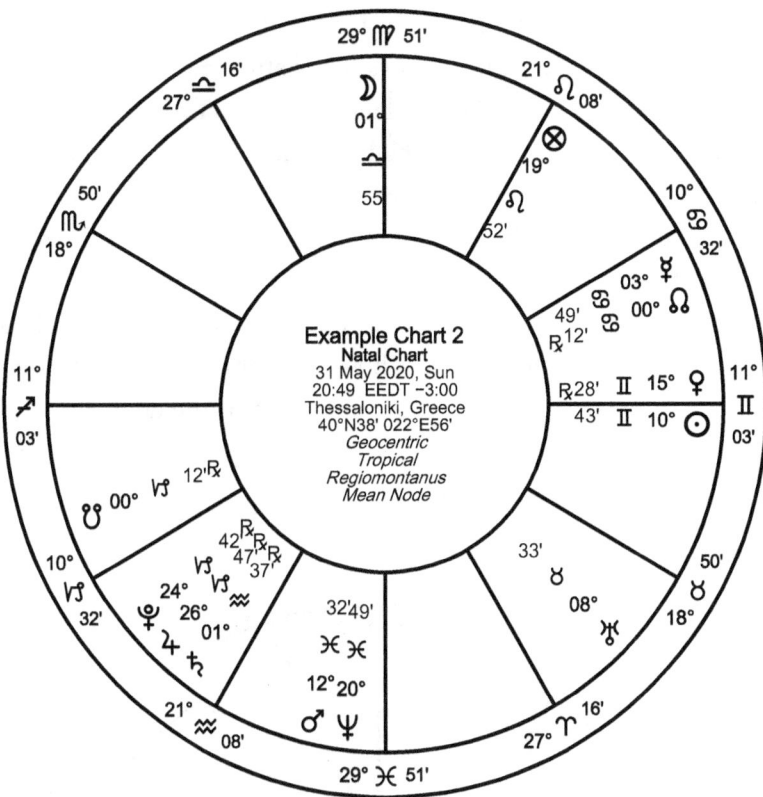

In this chart, calculated using the Regiomontanus house system, the MC is at 29°51′ Virgo and the Moon is in the 10th house but in Libra. If Libra were intercepted in the 10th house, then I would use the Moon and Venus (domicile ruler of Libra) as significators of 10th house matters along with Mercury, but Libra isn't intercepted in the 10th house. If Capricorn were the ascending sign, that would have made Libra the natural 10th sign from the ascendant, so in that case, I would also have used the Moon as a 10th house significator. As things are in the chart above, only Mercury can be used as a significator of 10th house matters, being the domicile ruler and the almuten of the 10th house and Virgo being the natural 10th sign when Sagittarius is rising. Lilly would have used both Mercury and Venus as 10th house rulers, because the 10th house is mostly comprised of degrees of the sign of Libra.

As for the rest of the planets in the above chart, the South Node, Jupiter and Pluto are in the 2nd house. Saturn can be regarded as a 3rd house planet or a 2nd house planet who aspects the ascendant and therefore is in a better position than Jupiter. Neptune is angular in the 4th house and I would also treat Mars as a 4th house planet. Uranus is placed in the 5th, but he is more of a 6th house planet as he doesn't aspect the ascendant. The Sun and Venus are 7th house planets and finally, Mercury and the North Node definitely belong to the 8th house. If there is a sign intercepted in a house and this sign is in its natural position in connection with the ascendant, then the domicile ruler of that sign is preferred to the ruler of the sign on the cusp, although I would suggest using both.

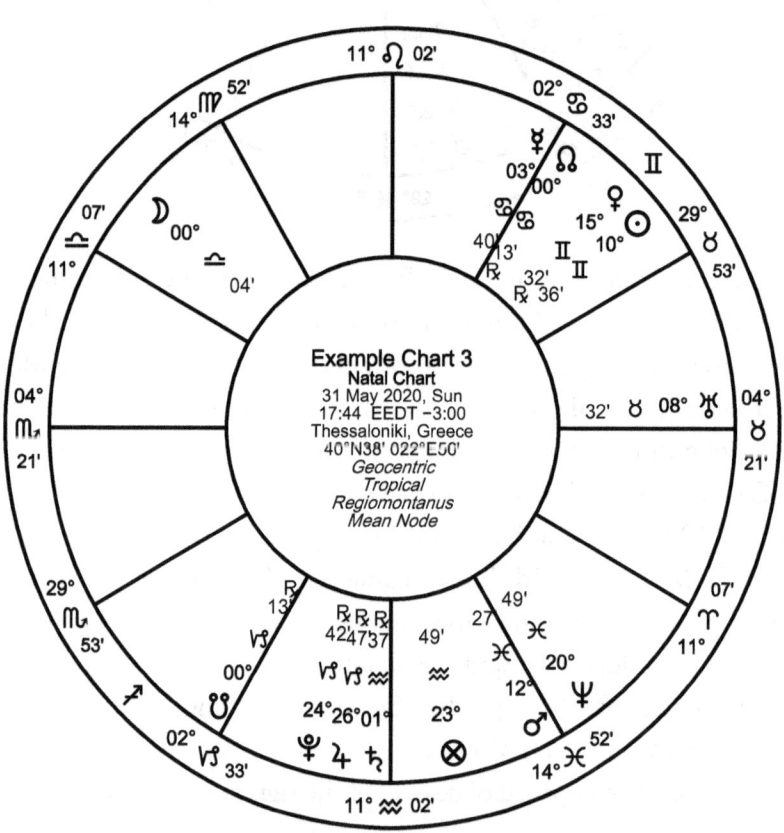

In Example Chart 3 calculated using the Regiomontanus house system, Sagittarius is intercepted in the 2nd house and Sagittarius is the natural second sign from the ascendant, so Jupiter, domicile ruler of Sagittarius, is the 2nd house preferred ruler, although Mars can be used as well.

The main significators in ANY horary chart are the ruler(s) of the ascendant and the Moon. In most charts you will get your answer if you check what is happening to them next. I believe that the ascendant does not really belong to the person asking the question, but to the question itself, so one must always check what happens to its ruler. Even if the querent is asking about a third party and the chart is fit to be judged, we would still check the ascendant ruler(s), because the person asking the question is deeply involved and if anything bad happens to their significators, then this is not good for the outcome of the question.

Don't make the mistake of treating the Moon as simply a co-significator of the querent. The Moon is the most important planetary body in a horary chart and she co-rules everything. If the Moon applies with a fortunate aspect with reception to the significator of the querent, this is very positive. It would be wrong to say that this is unimportant because one significator of the querent applies to the other, because the Moon is also co-significator of the quesited, whatever that may be. If the Moon applies with a hard aspect to an Infortune without a strong mutual reception and they are both essentially debilitated, the answer is almost always NO and you don't have to check anything else. It would take a rare chart with extremely fortunate indications that could make us overlook such a negative testimony.

I am strongly in favour of using house almutens, especially in nativities, but I think they have proven their validity in horary charts as well. A house almuten is the planet that has the most essential dignity in the degree of a cusp. The problem with almutens is that they can change depending on the house system one prefers, except for the angles of course, so I tend to use them as co-significators in angular houses mostly, unless of course the almuten is so obvious that whatever house system one uses, this cannot change. For example, house cusps in Libra and Aries in a diurnal chart always have Saturn and the Sun as their almutens (or co-almutens) respectively.

Finally, a planet that is located in the house we are interested in becomes automatically a co-significator with the ruler(s) of the cusp. Sometimes, this planet is more important than the rulers themselves, especially when the rulers do not aspect the house they rule. In the above chart, for example, Mars is conjunct the 5th house cusp in Pisces, so he is a significator of 5th house matters, along with Jupiter (domicile ruler and almuten).

To sum up, the significators of a house are: a) the domicile ruler of the sign on the cusp, b) the almuten or co-almuten (if two or more planets have the same score) of the sign on the cusp, mainly for angular houses ,c) the planet that is located inside the house and is in the same sign as the one on the cusp and d) the domicile ruler of the intercepted sign (if there is one) along with the planet(s) that might be located in the intercepted sign.

Relationship significators
The 1st house and its rulers for the querent and the 7th house and its rulers for the person of interest. A relationship question is not valid when there is no love interest in sight. Questions like: "When will I finally have a relationship?" are invalid and I would suggest the use of the nativity for this purpose and not a horary chart. The horary chart must be cast only when there is a love interest for someone else, who is already present in the life of the querent.

Even if you are asking about a third party, I would suggest you always check the radical 1st and 7th houses together with the derived ones. Do not use the Sun for men and Venus for women as co-significators, because they may signify a third person, unless it is certain that no third person is involved. Instead, use Venus for love in general. If the Moon is applying to Venus with a fortunate aspect and there is also reception, this is very good testimony. Mars in the 7th almost always indicates breakup or divorce. Although the outers should be avoided in general, I've noticed that Uranus close to the 7th house cusp or in a conjunction with the Moon is also negative testimony.

I would suggest always using the 7th house for relationship questions and do not make a distinction between sexual affairs and relationships, by using the 5th house for sexual affairs. Al Biruni and Masha'allah consider the 7th house to be the house of sexual unions. The 5th house, by being the house Venus naturally rules and also rejoices in, may have something to do with sex, but with sex as an act, and it cannot signify a person to have sex with. It is the same thing as a bet, also ruled by the 5th house. The fact that the querent's significators apply to the significators of the bet doesn't mean that they won – you want the significators of money for this. Now, if the question is indeed only about sex, what can the question be if there is no other person involved? "When will I have sex again?", for example? This is an invalid question, because there is no connection with the present. If there is someone in the picture that you could potentially have sex with, then you go to the 7th house.

Job significators
Use the 10th house for most questions about work, especially if the question is "Will I get this job I applied for?", because success is also involved in this question and worldly success belongs to the 10th house. Your boss is also here while your equal in rank co-workers belong to the 7th house. People who work for you, that is, you are their employer, are usually assigned to the 6th house, especially if we are talking about house servants, gardeners etc. Labourers in general belong to the 6th house as well.

Health significators
The querent's health, their body is the 1st house. The rulers of the 1st house will determine the state of health of the querent, along with the Moon. Illness belongs to the 6th house in general, but the cause of the querent's illness in most horary charts is the planets that are afflicting

the ascendant, its rulers and the Moon. I would strongly suggest that you do NOT make a diagnosis based on a horary chart, because you are not a doctor. Limit yourself to saying whether the querent is going to get better or not. If the querent's significators are about to make fortunate aspects with reception, then they are going to get better. If they are about to make unfortunate aspects without reception, then they are going to get worse. Death belongs to the 8th house and its significators, although hard aspects to Mars and Saturn without a strong mutual reception can also signify death. If the question is about a third party, the derived 8th house and its rulers can also be used as significators of death. For example, if the question is about the health of a 7th house person, the 2nd house (8th house from the 7th) can also signify death (along with the radical 8th house).

Money significators
The 2nd house is the house of money. Don't go searching around the chart for specific significators. Is the question about you getting some money? Then, the 2nd house is the house you are looking for. It doesn't matter where the money comes from. Whether it is money from a bet, money from the government, money from whoever, the main thing here is if the money is going to come to YOU. So if the 2nd house ruler is afflicted, this is bad testimony and it often is the only testimony you'll need. However, you can have a look at the 8th house for other people's money (winnings from bets, loans) and the 11th house for money from government in cases where things are unclear. If it is a third party question, always use the derived 2nd house for that person's money. For example, if the question is about the father, then his money belongs to the 5th house (2nd from the 4th).

Questions about sport/elections
These questions are only valid if they are about a team, a player or a candidate/party you support. Remember, if you want to place a bet, asking about if your team will win is wrong, because that is not what you want

to know, the bet is what interests you. The 1st house goes to the team or the player you support, because you identify with them, and the 10th house goes to the win. The same goes for elections, the 1st house goes to the candidate you support and the 10th house to the win. The fixed star Regulus seems to be quite important in such charts and can outweigh some negative testimony elsewhere if it is conjunct the 1st or the 10th house cusp or makes a conjunction with the rulers of those angles.

Questions about thefts/missing items/missing pets etc.
Don't play detective. Lilly enjoyed doing that, but going around London searching for your stolen fish is not something I would recommend. With your own questions, you can play all the games you want, but if you are doing client work, limit yourself to saying if the client is going to find the thing stolen or missing. If you start saying things like: "The missing item is north by northwest near water or a heat source of some kind", this is not going to help the client much and, don't forget, the item will be found when it is meant to be found, despite your valiant efforts for immediate recovery. Stick to the basic rule: Are your main significators applying to fortunate aspects with reception in fortunate houses? The querent will find the missing item. If not, the item won't be found. Olivia Barclay also used the 4th house regarding where to look for an object that is not lost, but definitely mislaid. For pets, always use the radical 6th house and don't turn the chart if it's a third party question.

Questions about books/publishing
If you plan to write a book, first of all do not ask: "If I write a book, will it be published?" This is another "Should I?" question, therefore invalid. Books, in general, belong to the 9th house, as a source of higher knowledge, but your book is not a source of higher knowledge for you. It's your way of communicating and expressing yourself, so I would place it in the 3rd house. Placing your book in the 5th house, as your creation, is not entirely devoid of sense, but I prefer the 3rd house, because I find it difficult to liken a book to a child. Anyway, if you are asking: "Will

the book I'm writing be published?", what you are really asking is: "Will I sign a contract with a publishing house?", so this is more a 1st/7th house issue than a 3rd/9th (publishing house) one. The 3rd and 9th house significators are of secondary importance.

Questions about cars
In general, cars belong to the 3rd house, but I fail to see which sort of context would make one use the 3rd house for cars in a horary question. If the question is about a trip and whether it is safe or not, then the house that matters is the 1st one. Even if you ask something like: "My car is in a bad condition, will it make it on a road trip?", what you are really interested in is if you will make the trip and the 3rd house may not be necessary, although it can be used for additional information in this case. If the question is about buying or selling a car, the 2nd house is more important.

Questions about parents
Both Mum and Dad are included in the 4th house, which represents the family as a unit. The Sun (Dad) is the natural ruler of the 4th house and Cancer (Mum) is the sign that is associated with it. In many cases, though, we need to make a distinction between Dad and Mum and according to the tradition, Dad belongs to the 4th house and Mum to the 10th, as the 7th from the 4th house (Dad's wife). Furthermore, the Sun and Venus are said to rule Dad and Mum in diurnal charts and Saturn and the Moon in nocturnal charts. I'm not entirely convinced by either of the two distinctions. I would prefer Mum and Dad to be always ruled by the Sun and the Moon in all charts and this Dad's wife thing is not very appealing. I would therefore suggest to also try the domicile rulers of the Lot of Father (Asc+Saturn–Sun, reversed in nocturnal charts) and the Lot of Mother (Asc+Moon–Venus, reversed in nocturnal charts). So if the ruler of the Lot of Mother, for example, coincides with the ruler of the 10th house, then this is the planet that most likely represents her the most.

Questions about court cases

The querent gets the 1st house as always, the adversary belongs to the 7th house, the judge is the 10th house and the end of the matter is signified by the 4th house. I suggest you treat this as a 1st/7th house issue and leave the 10th and 4th house out of this because they usually complicate things. If you check the querent's significators and what happens to them next, you will almost always get your answer. Remember, we try to avoid writing film scripts and we don't want the full story. Who wins, that's all we need to know. Leave the rest of the details to the court's ruling.

Questions about friends

It is the 7th house that shows sociable or unsociable people, not the 11th. The 11th house should be reserved for that small number of people you can trust completely and can count on in hours of need. Common friends and acquaintances belong to the 7th house.

General meanings of houses for most common horary questions

1st house = the querent, the body, health
2nd house = money, moveable goods
3rd house = siblings, cousins, peers, ways of communication
4th house = parents (the father, mostly), real estate
5th house = children, places of entertainment
6th house = illness, small animals, labourers
7th house = spouse/love interest, contracts, disputes, thieves
8th house = death, loans, other people's money
9th house = foreign travel, religion, higher education
10th house = work, boss, success, win
11th house = very close friends, hope, trust, ambition
12th house = self-undoing, imprisonment, unknown enemies,
        large animals

Tip: Don't go around searching for significators for the most trivial things. It is a wide misconception these days that you need to find a house for everything and people are saying what a pity it is that the world has changed so much since Lilly's day, who couldn't possibly assign things to houses to meet today's needs. Don't fret. The most important significators, I repeat, in ANY horary chart are the rulers of the ascendant and the Moon. If these significators apply to form fortunate aspects with reception, you will most likely get/have the quesited in whatever house the latter may belong to. If not, you won't. It is a rare chart that can go against this very basic rule and when it does, the chart is most likely invalid. More about this in later chapters.

STEP THREE

ASSESSING THE SIGNIFICATORS

OUR SIGNIFICATORS ARE ASSESSED in three ways. First, we examine the sign or the part of the sign they are in to check if it suits them (essential dignities), then we check their location in the chart and the relationship they have with other planets (accidental dignities) and finally we check whether they can offer help to one another (receptions).

Essential dignities

Planets have domiciles, signs where they feel like home, that is. All planets have two domiciles and the Lights have one. The domiciles of Saturn are Capricorn and Aquarius, the domiciles of Jupiter are Sagittarius and Pisces, the domiciles of Mars are Aries and Scorpio, the domicile of the Sun is Leo, the domiciles of Venus are Taurus and Libra, the domiciles of Mercury are Gemini and Virgo and the domicile of the Moon is Cancer. The opposite signs of their domiciles are said to be places of great debility for the planets. We say that Saturn is in detriment in Cancer and Leo, Jupiter in Gemini and Virgo, Mars in Taurus and Libra, the Sun in Aquarius, Venus in Aries and Scorpio, Mercury in Sagittarius and Pisces and the Moon in Capricorn.

Score: *A planet in domicile gets 5 points. This score will be used in order to find the almuten.*

The second strongest dignity is exaltation. Planets have signs which may not feel like home, but they are like honoured guests there. Saturn is exalted in Libra, Jupiter in Cancer, Mars in Capricorn, the Sun in Aries, Venus in Pisces, Mercury in Virgo (also his domicile) and the Moon in Taurus. The sign opposite a planet's exaltation is where the planet is in its fall, a negative testimony. Saturn is in fall in Aries, Jupiter in

Capricorn, Mars in Cancer, the Sun in Libra, Venus in Virgo, Mercury in Pisces (also his detriment) and the Moon in Scorpio.

Score: *A planet in exaltation gets 4 points.*

Each sign belongs to a triplicity of signs based on the element of their nature. There are four elements in astrology. Fire (Aries, Leo, Sagittarius), Earth (Taurus, Virgo, Capricorn), Air (Gemini, Libra, Aquarius) and Water (Cancer, Scorpio, Pisces). Each triplicity has a different ruler in a day chart (diurnal) than in a night (nocturnal) chart. A day chart is a chart with the Sun above the horizon, that is, above the 1st/7th house axis, in houses 12, 11, 10, 9, 8, 7. A night chart is a chart with the Sun below the horizon, that is, below the 1st/7th house axis, in houses 6, 5, 4, 3, 2, 1. Planets in fire signs in a diurnal chart have the Sun as triplicity ruler and in a nocturnal chart, Jupiter. Planets in earth signs in a diurnal chart have Venus as triplicity ruler and in a nocturnal chart, the Moon. Planets in air signs in a diurnal chart have Saturn as triplicity ruler and in a nocturnal chart, Mercury. Finally, planets in water signs in a diurnal chart have Venus as triplicity ruler and in a nocturnal chart, Mars. As you may have deduced by now, I use the Dorothean triplicity rulers and not those of Ptolemy, because to have Mars both as diurnal and nocturnal ruler in the water signs is nonsensical to say the least.

Score: *A planet being in its own triplicity gets 3 points.*

In every sign there are certain degrees that each planet (with the exception of the Lights) finds itself quite comfortable in. Each sign is divided into five unequal parts and the five traditional planets are said to rule such a part in every sign. These parts are called terms or bounds. Each one of the five traditional planets (Saturn, Jupiter, Mars, Venus, Mercury) rules one such unequal part in every sign and if they find themselves there, then they have some dignity and we say that the planet is in its own terms. I personally use the Egyptian terms and not the Ptolemaic ones, because I don't find Ptolemy's story believable about how he came across them. The table below shows the Egyptian terms. I will explain how to read it, because it is this table that students have most trouble reading, in either the Egyptian or the Ptolemaic form.

The Egyptian Terms

S	1		2		3		4		5	
♈	♃	6	♀	6 (12)	☿	8 (20)	♂	5 (25)	♄	5 (30)
♉	♀	8	☿	6 (14)	♃	8 (22)	♄	5 (27)	♂	3 (30)
♊	☿	6	♃	6 (12)	♀	5 (17)	♂	7 (24)	♄	6 (30)
♋	♂	7	♀	6 (13)	☿	6 (19)	♃	7 (26)	♄	4 (30)
♌	♃	6	♀	5 (11)	♄	7 (18)	☿	6 (24)	♂	6 (30)
♍	☿	7	♀	10 (17)	♃	4 (21)	♂	7 (28)	♄	2 (30)
♎	♄	6	☿	8 (14)	♃	7 (21)	♀	7 (28)	♂	2 (30)
♏	♂	7	♀	4 (11)	☿	8 (19)	♃	5 (24)	♄	6 (30)
♐	♃	12	♀	5 (17)	☿	4 (21)	♄	5 (26)	♂	4 (30)
♑	☿	7	♃	7 (14)	♀	8 (22)	♄	4 (26)	♂	4 (30)
♒	☿	7	♀	6 (13)	♃	7 (20)	♂	5 (25)	♄	5 (30)
♓	♀	12	♃	4 (16)	☿	3 (19)	♂	9 (28)	♄	2 (30)

In the first row, we have the terms of the sign of Aries. You can see the Aries symbol on the left. The planet that rules the first unequal part of Aries is Jupiter. The number next to Jupiter is the number of degrees that Jupiter rules, the first six degrees in particular. This means that Jupiter rules the Aries degrees from 0°00′ to 5°59′. In the next column, we see Venus, who rules the second unequal part in Aries. We see that she also rules six degrees (the first number beside her), until the 12th degree of Aries (the number in brackets); that is, she rules from 6°00′ to 11°59′ of Aries. Next in line is Mercury, who rules 8 degrees in Aries until the number of 20; that is, he rules from 12°00′ to 19°59′ of Aries and so forth. So if you want, for example, to find in whose terms a planet at 21°17′ Leo is, you go to the Leo row where you see that the first six degrees are ruled by Jupiter, then Venus becomes the term ruler until the

11th degree, then it's Saturn's turn until the 18th degree and Mercury's turn until the 24th degree. Your planet is at 21°17′ Leo, that is, between the 18th degree and the 24th degree. Mercury rules the part in Leo from 18°00′ to 23°59′, so your planet is in the terms of Mercury.

Now, why do I say 5°59′, for example, and not 6°00′, like I see many astrologers suggest? Because, if you see the end number of each row, that number is 30. There is no 30; 30 is in fact 0°00′ of the next sign, where the term ruler changes. The planet that rules the last unequal part of each sign ends its rulership at 29°59′. So, if there is no 30, then there can be no 6.

The terms are considered a minor dignity, but I believe that they are very important, especially in natal work. Lilly gave two points to a planet in its own terms, but I consider terms even stronger than triplicity when it comes to dignities.

Score: A planet being in its own terms gets 2 points.

The final form of dignity is face, the weakest of them all. Again, the signs have been divided, but now in three equal parts of 10 degrees each and the Lights have been reinserted as rulers. The first face of Aries (0°00′ to 09°59′) is assigned to Mars, who is the domicile ruler of Aries. From then on, the planets that rule the faces follow the Chaldean order of planets (Saturn, Jupiter, Mars, the Sun, Venus, Mercury, the Moon). So the second face of Aries is ruled by the Sun, who is next in line after Mars in the Chaldean order of planets, the third face of Aries is ruled by Venus; the first face of Taurus is ruled by Mercury, the second face of Taurus is ruled by the Moon, the third face of Taurus is ruled by Saturn and so forth.

Score: Lilly gives one point for a planet in its own face. The face dignity is very weak and can safely be ignored in general, unless another form of dignity is also present and face strengthens it a little more.

Sign	Houses of the Planets		Exalt-ation	Triplicity of Planets		The Terms of the Planets										The Faces of the Planets			Detri ment	Fall
				D	N															
♈	♂	D	☉ 19	☉	♃	♃	6	♀	6 (12)	☿	8 (20)	♂	5 (25)	♄	5 (30)	♂ 10	☉ 20	♀ 30	♀	♄
♉	♀	N	☽ 3	♀	☽	♀	8	☿	6 (14)	♃	8 (22)	♄	5 (27)	♂	3 (30)	☿ 10	☽ 20	♄ 30	♂	
♊	☿	D	☊ 3	♄	☿	☿	6	♃	6 (12)	♀	5 (17)	♂	7 (24)	♄	6 (30)	♃ 10	♂ 20	☉ 30	♃	
♋	☽	D/N	♃ 15	♀	♂	♂	7	♀	6 (13)	☿	6 (19)	♃	7 (26)	♄	4 (30)	♀ 10	☿ 20	☽ 30	♄	♂
♌	☉	D/N		☉	♃	♃	6	♀	5 (11)	♄	7 (18)	☿	6 (24)	♂	6 (30)	♄ 10	♃ 20	♂ 30	♄	
♍	☿	N	☿ 15	♀	☽	☿	7	♀	10 (17)	♃	4 (21)	♂	7 (28)	♄	2 (30)	☉ 10	♀ 20	☿ 30	♃	♀
♎	♀	D	♄ 21	♄	☿	♄	6	☿	8 (14)	♃	7 (21)	♀	7 (28)	♂	2 (30)	☽ 10	♄ 20	♃ 30	♂	☉
♏	♂	N		♀	♂	♂	7	♀	4 (11)	☿	8 (19)	♃	5 (24)	♄	6 (30)	♂ 10	☉ 20	♀ 30	♀	☽
♐	♃	D	☋ 3	☉	♃	♃	12	♀	5 (17)	☿	4 (21)	♄	5 (26)	♂	4 (30)	☿ 10	☽ 20	♄ 30	☿	
♑	♄	N	♂ 28	♀	☽	☿	7	♃	7 (14)	♀	8 (22)	♄	4 (26)	♂	4 (30)	♃ 10	♂ 20	☉ 30	☽	♃
♒	♄	D		♄	☿	☿	7	♀	6 (13)	♃	7 (20)	♂	5 (25)	♄	5 (30)	♀ 10	☿ 20	☽ 30	☉	
♓	♃	N	♀ 27	♀	♂	♀	12	♃	4 (16)	☿	3 (19)	♂	9 (28)	♄	2 (30)	♄ 10	♃ 20	♂ 30	☿	☿

Table of essential dignities using the Dorothean triplicity rulers and the Egyptian terms

In some cases, a planet has both essential dignity and debility. When these two collide, it is always essential dignity that wins, unless it's only by face in which case debility prevails. Venus in Virgo, for example, in a diurnal chart is also in her triplicity and in her fall. Some people say that since fall gets –4 in Lilly's scoring system and triplicity gets +3, then we can call this Venus weak. Personally, I don't think that it works that way, because we don't do maths in astrology. The important thing is for a planet to have dignity. If this happens, debility falls by the wayside. Venus in Virgo is in a hostile place, but if she is in her triplicity or terms, she is at the safest part of that hostile place. This is enough for her to function adequately.

See p.29 for a full table of essential dignities with the Dorothean triplicity rulers and the Egyptian terms.

A couple of examples
a) a planet at 12° Libra in a nocturnal chart is in the domicile of Venus, in the exaltation of Saturn, in the triplicity of Mercury, in the terms of Mercury and in the face of Saturn.

b) a planet at 26° Aquarius in a diurnal chart is in the domicile of Saturn, in the triplicity of Saturn, in the terms of Saturn and in the face of the Moon.

With essential dignity, we are interested in two things: a) whether a planet has some dignity of its own and b) in what other planets' dignities our planet is. For example, Mercury at 18° Scorpio is in his own terms and this strengthens him, because Scorpio is not one of his "good" signs (domicile, exaltation). Mercury in Scorpio is also in the domicile of Mars. If Mars and Mercury make a fortunate applying aspect, this will help Mercury, because Mars will receive him. Finally, if Mars is also in one or more of Mercury's dignities, then the reception is mutual and this helps Mercury a lot. More about reception further down.

Step Three – Assessing the Significators

The almuten of a house is the planet that has the most dignity (the best overall score) in the degree on the cusp of a house. In the first example above (12° Libra), Venus gets five points from domicile, Mercury also gets five points (3 from triplicity and 2 from the terms) and finally Saturn also gets 5 points (4 from exaltation and 1 from face). This means that all three of them are co-almutens of the house with 12° Libra on the cusp in a nocturnal chart.

In the second example, Saturn obviously gets the most points (9 total) and besides being the domicile ruler, he is also the almuten of the house with 26° Aquarius on the cusp. In my practice, I use both the domicile ruler and the almuten of an angular house as significators.

Before we move on to receptions, let's talk a little bit about aspects, because we will need them for explaining what receptions do. An aspect is a relationship two signs have if they are a certain number of degrees apart. If they are 60 degrees apart, the aspect is called a sextile. For example, Aries and Gemini form a sextile aspect, because each degree of Aries is 60 degrees apart from the same degree in Gemini. **It must be noted that the whole of Aries forms a sextile with the whole of Gemini even if we are talking about the 1st degree of Aries and the 30th of Gemini.**

Signs that are 90 degrees apart, e.g. Aries and Cancer, form an aspect of a 90–degree distance called square. Signs that are 120 degrees apart, e.g. Aries and Leo, form an aspect of a 120–degree distance called trine. Finally, signs that are opposite one another, 180 degrees apart, e.g. Aries and Libra, form an opposition aspect. Planets found in those signs are said to be involved in an aspect according to the sign they are in. For example, a planet in Aries and a planet in Leo form a trine aspect. If they are in the same degree of their respective signs, the aspect is called partill or partile, in other words exact. If the faster planet is behind in degrees from the slower planet and it's catching up, then we say that the aspect is applying. If the faster planet is ahead in degrees from the slower planet and the more it moves, the longer the distance between the two, then we say that the aspect is separating. Applying aspects in horary show future events and separating aspects show past events.

There is another relationship between planets that is technically not an aspect, but is treated like one and that is the conjunction, two planets being in the same sign. The conjunction is considered to be the most powerful of all relationships between planets.

Now, for an aspect to exist, we only need the two (or more) planets to be in the appropriate signs regardless of degrees. A planet at 1° Scorpio is conjunct a planet at 29° Scorpio and a planet in 2° Leo forms a trine with a planet at 22° Sagittarius. However, those aspects that are formed by planets so far from the exact number of degrees that determines the aspect (e.g. 120° degrees for a trine or 90° degrees for a square) are hardly effective, so the notion of orbs was introduced. Lilly included in his work a table of orbs for every planet (not all planets have the same orb), which you can find on the Internet. What he did was add the orbs of the two planets and divided the total in half (moiety). So if a planet has, let's say, an orb of 8 degrees and the other planet has an orb of 12 degrees, the aspect between these two is effective with an orb of 10 degrees (12+8/2) or less. I can't say for certain that wide orbs are completely ineffective, but personally I don't trust wider than 12 degree orbs or thereabouts for any planet and especially for the Moon, who I now consider void of course when that happens, especially if she is more than 15 degrees away from her next aspect.

Receptions

We've seen that every planet in the chart is located in someone else's dignities or, hopefully, in some of its own. The planets which have power (dignity) in these places are called dispositors. So Mercury, for example, at 2° Aries in a nocturnal chart has Mars as domicile ruler, the Sun as exaltation ruler, Jupiter as triplicity ruler, Jupiter again as term ruler (Egyptian) and Mars again as face ruler. These three planets (Mars, the Sun and Jupiter) are called Mercury's dispositors and we say that they

RECEIVE him, which means that they are in a position to help him if some criteria are met:

a) Mercury is in the same sign as his dispositor, who is in his domicile or exaltation. If, for example, Mars is also in Aries, then Mars receives Mercury and the help is significant. This is the best possible single reception (when only one planet does the receiving). In this case, we do not need Mercury to apply to Mars, it's enough that they both are in Mars' sign. This is very strong, except perhaps in cases where the received planet is in its detriment or fall, for example the Moon or Jupiter in Capricorn and Saturn also in Capricorn. Saturn receives them, but it is as if the Moon or Jupiter completely surrender to the enemy. Saturn may offer help, but this help feels more like imprisonment. If this happens in Aquarius or Libra, it's much better.

b) There is a fortunate (trine/sextile) applying aspect between Mercury and one (or more) of his dispositors. These dispositors will help Mercury and this is a fortunate testimony in any chart.

c) There is an unfortunate (opposition/square) applying aspect between Mercury and those of his dispositors that are Fortunes (Jupiter or Venus. Naturally, Mercury can never make an opposition with Venus). In our example, Mercury is in the dignities of Mars, the Sun and Jupiter and the only Fortune between them is Jupiter. If Mercury applies with a hard aspect to the Sun or Mars, the single reception is not enough to produce a succesful outcome. If, however, he applies to Jupiter, then not everything is lost. It may not be the best of testimonies, but if the Fortune (Jupiter in this case) is in a very good condition, i.e. with lots of essential dignity, we can still have a positive outcome if other testimonies also agree. I must say, though, that the opposition is always problematic and besides essential dignity, we would also need a third planet that aspects both opposing planets with a trine and a sextile, preferably with reception.

If the applying aspect has only reception with face, it can safely be ignored. Not much help there. If the aspect with the dispositor is separating, a single reception is almost always negligible. It can be of some help and should perhaps be noted when the aspect is very close and it is the last aspect our planet made. If our planet applies with a hard aspect to an Infortune (Mars/Saturn) or the Sun, this is very negative testimony and the presence of a single reception is almost never enough to produce a succesful outcome.

When a planet is in none of its own dignites, like Mercury is in our example, then we say that the planet is peregrine. Lilly thought this is a very serious weakness and gave a peregrine planet a score of minus five. However, I think that if the planet in question applies to another planet who receives it with any dignity other than face, peregrine status can safely be ignored.

When a dispositor of our planet is also in a dignity of our planet, then we say that the reception is mutual. So if Mercury, like we've already said, is in the domicile and face of Mars and Mars is, let's say, at 18° Cancer in the terms of Mercury, then the reception is mutual and they both receive each other. Mutual reception doesn't usually require an aspect (although some people disagree with this) and both planets are significantly helped. Naturally, the stronger the dignity, the better. We can stop worrying about a square with a Fortune if the reception is mutual (the opposition is always worrisome) or even squares or conjunctions with Infortunes when the mutual reception is between domicile and exaltation, e.g. Venus and Saturn conjunct in Libra or the Moon in Aries square Mars in Cancer.

Here are some chart examples:

Reception Chart 1: Jupiter is in Aquarius in the domicile and triplicity (diurnal chart) of Saturn. Jupiter doesn't receive Saturn because Saturn is in none of the dignities of Jupiter. This is the strongest possible single reception, that is the reception by conjunction. Saturn is inside his own

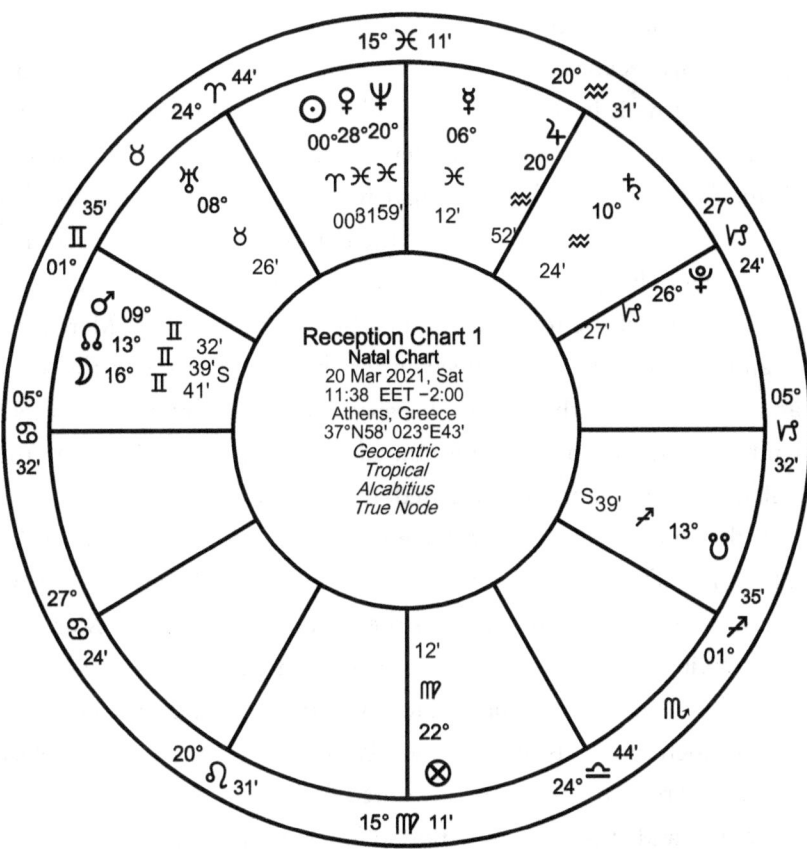

house and will protect his guest Jupiter from the enemies, provided, of course, Jupiter abides by Saturn's rules. In Aquarius, a hot and moist sign, Saturn is more flexible and less strict and severe as in his other domicile, the sign of Capricorn. The same reception also happened the previous year in Capricorn, but Capricorn is a very unfriendly place for Jupiter. The kind of help that Saturn offered (because he did offer help) to Jupiter in Capricorn was against Jupiter's nature and much less appreciated.

In the same chart, we have another reception of the same nature. Mercury in Pisces is received by conjunction by Venus in Pisces, where she is exalted (Mercury is also in the triplicity and terms of Venus). It doesn't matter, I repeat, if the planets apply or separate, all that's required in the reception by conjunction is that they are in the same sign. Mercury receives lots of help from Venus and we can safely ignore the fact that he is in detriment and fall, because unlike in the previous example, Venus is a Fortune and Mercury and Venus are not enemies by nature. However, he applies to a square with Mars. Mercury receives Mars and is willing to offer some help, but the nature of the aspect is such that little actual help can be received. However, Mars is not harmed by this aspect because of the reception and because of the fact that Mercury is not an Infortune. He is not helped either, though. Mercury, on the other hand, is harmed by this square, because Mars is an Infortune without dignity and the reception is not mutual. If Mercury and Mars were the significators for querent and quesited, the answer would be NO.

In the same chart, we also have an applying aspect between Mars and Saturn. The aspect is a trine and no reception is needed, but we do have one nonetheless. Saturn is the triplicity dispositor of Mars and Mars applies to him, so Saturn receives and helps Mars adequately, especially by being in Aquarius. However, they are both in bad houses (even though Saturn is in the same sign as the 9th house cusp, I place him in the 8th house where he is located, because he doesn't aspect the ascendant) and this trine may not suffice for a positive outcome and we may need help from other chart factors. Now, if Mercury managed to catch up with Mars before Mars forms the trine to Saturn, the trine would be hindered, but as it stands, Mars will first contact Saturn and not Mercury.

Step Three – Assessing the Significators

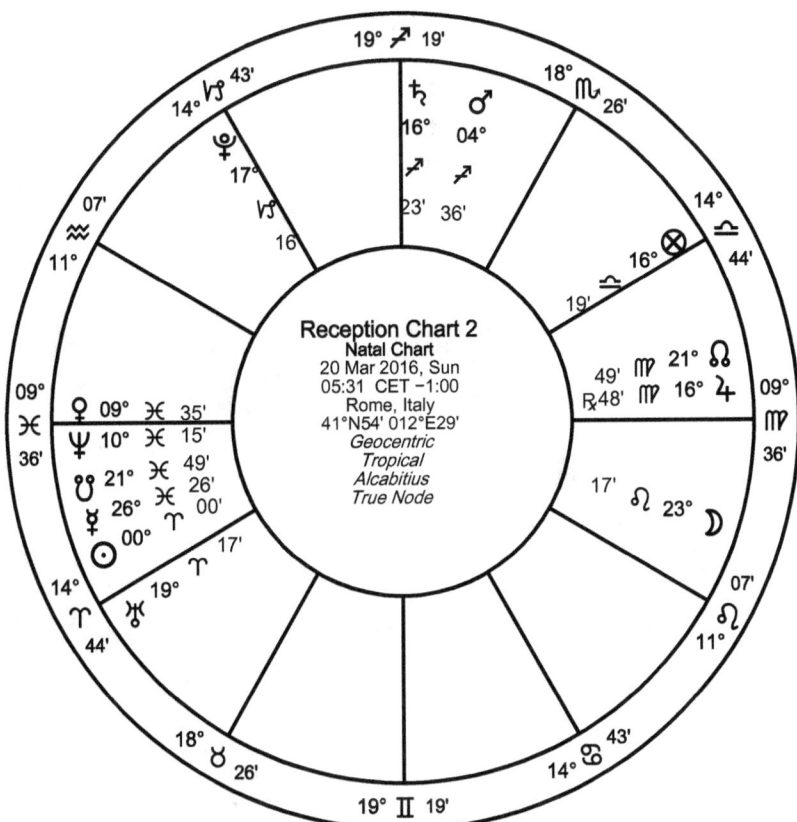

Reception Chart 2: Jupiter may be in fall and retrograde, but receives help from Mercury (mutual reception by domicile, but the aspect is an opposition and the help is therefore limited), who, in turn, is greatly helped by angular Venus in Pisces (reception by conjunction). Jupiter, however, applies to a square with Saturn. Saturn is in Jupiter's domicile and Jupiter receives him, but we are talking about a square with an Infortune and we would have needed a mutual reception by domicile or exaltation. If Jupiter and Saturn were our main significators, the answer would be NO.

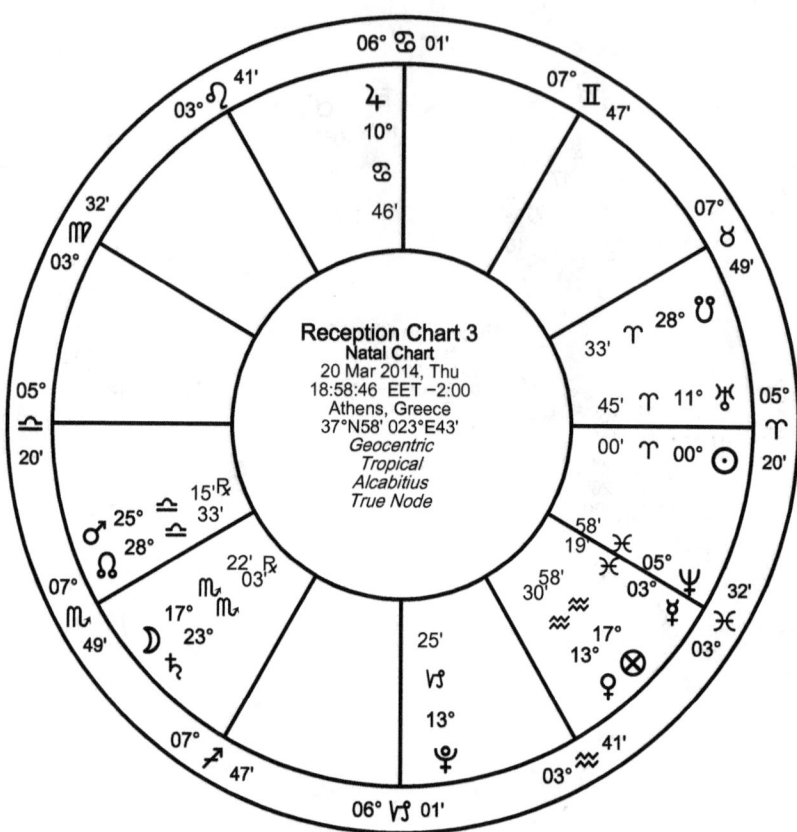

Reception Chart 3: A reception, single or mutual, is always more than welcome, but in some cases the help offered is weak. This is one of those cases. Mars is in the exaltation of Saturn and Saturn is in the domicile and triplicity of Mars. This kind of mutual reception is usually very strong, but in this case the planets are both retrograde and Infortunes, they do not aspect each other (an aspect is not needed for a mutual reception, but naturally it strengthens it a lot) and Mars is in detriment. Neither planet can expect significant help from the other.

Step Three – Assessing the Significators

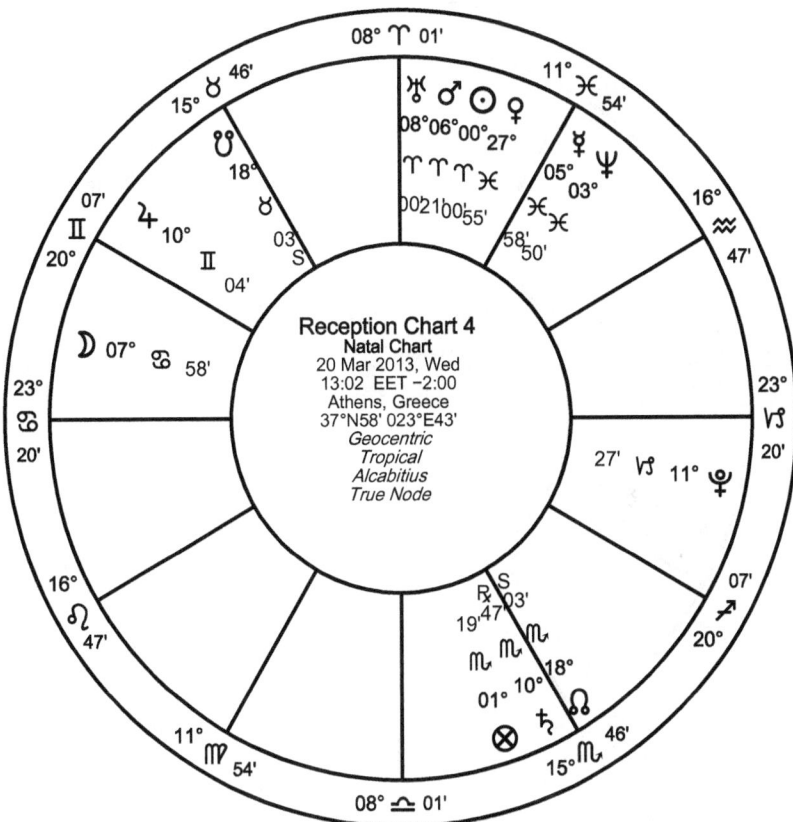

Reception Chart 4: Mercury and Jupiter are in mutual reception by domicile. This is not the same case as the previous example. Jupiter is a Fortune and Mercury is not an Infortune, they aspect one another (Mercury's next aspect is a trine to Saturn, but trines cannot hinder anything) and neither planet is retrograde. Still, the aspect is a square and they are both in detriment. If these two planets were our main significators, the answer wouldn't be an automatic YES and the rest of the chart factors would have to be examined.

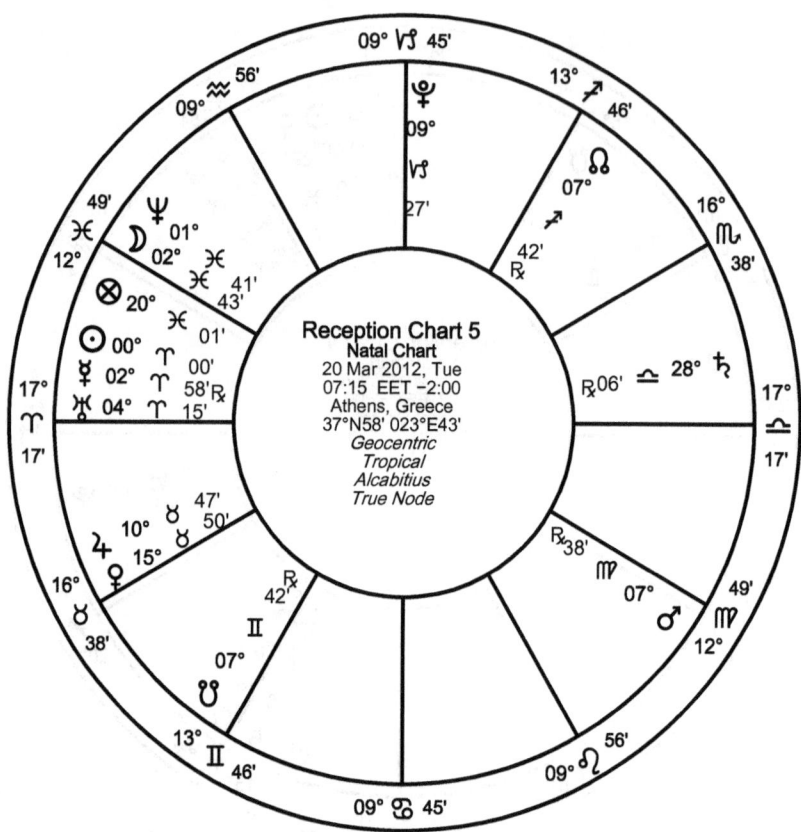

Reception Chart 5: The Moon and Jupiter are in a very strong mutual reception between domicile and exaltation and this is very fortunate. Sadly, Jupiter is not the Moon's next aspect, but she applies to an opposition with Mars, a retrograde Infortune. If the Moon and Mars had had a strong mutual reception and given the fact that Jupiter and Venus help the opposing planets by sextiling and trining them, perhaps the opposition could have been saved. The way things are, the sextile between the Moon and Jupiter is hindered by Mars and the answer, whatever the question might be, would be NO, with Mars also being the domicile ruler of the ascendant. Needless to say that Mars can hardly be helped by his mutual reception with retrograde and combust Mercury.

Step Three – Assessing the Significators 41

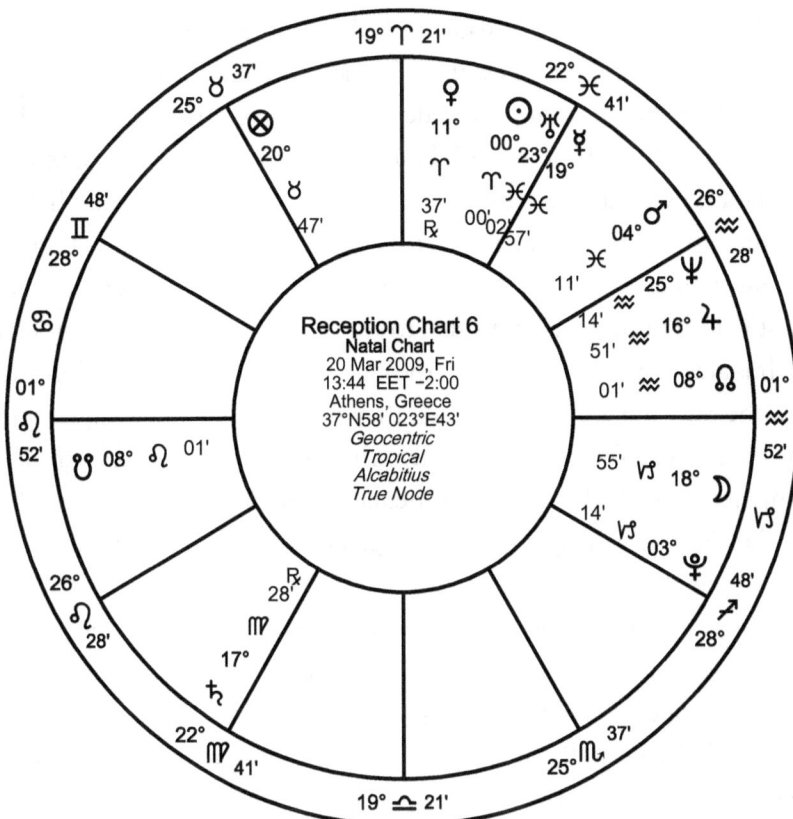

Reception Chart 6: The Moon in Capricorn applies to a sextile with Mercury in Pisces. The sextile is a fortunate aspect, but because it's weaker than the trine, it usually needs at least a single reception to give a positive outcome, unless both planets are essentially strong. Here, both the Moon and Mercury are essentially debilitated and therefore the sextile is not enough.

Accidental dignities

This is another form of dignity and it has nothing to do with signs, but mainly about a planet's location in a chart and its relationship with other planets.

First of all, as we've already said, the good houses for a planet to be in are the angular houses, the 5th and the 11th house. The rest are weak, either because they are cadent (falling from the angles in other words), like the 3rd and the 9th house, or because they don't aspect the ascendant by nature, like the 2nd and the 8th house. The worst houses are the 6th and the 12th because they are both cadent and don't aspect the ascendant by nature. This is the rule, but, as I said in step two, one must really check the planet's sign to see if it aspects the ascending sign.

It is always a good thing when the planets trine or sextile the Fortunes and the Sun and a bad thing when they oppose, conjunct or square the Infortunes and the Sun, especially when there is no reception. The conjunction with the Sun in particular is very serious and it is called combustion. This happens when the planet is up to 8 or 8°30′ minutes away from the Sun, either before or after it. When the planet is too close to the Sun, no more than 17′ away, then, surprisingly enough, this is considered to be very fortunate and it is called cazimi. Some authors want the planet to be on the ecliptic at the moment of the cazimi, not just on the same zodiacal degree, meaning that it must have no more than 17′ of latitude. They have a point. Planets that are less than 17° away from the Sun, but more than 8°, are not combust, but they are said to be under the beams, which is also a debility – less serious than combustion, though.

Following the above logic, it's always good for planets to be far from the Sun. Superior planets (Mars, Jupiter, Saturn) are happier when they are oriental, that is, behind the Sun in zodiacal degrees, because, as the Sun is faster than them, the more he moves, the further away from them he goes. In contrast, inferior planets (Mercury and Venus) are better when they are occidental, because they are usually faster than the Sun and when they are occidental, they are moving away from him. As for the Moon, she also needs to be moving away from the Sun, so she is better when she is occidental, in other words increasing in light. She is increasing in light from the moment of the conjunction (New Moon) up until the opposition (Full Moon). After the Full Moon, she is decreasing

Step Three – Assessing the Significators

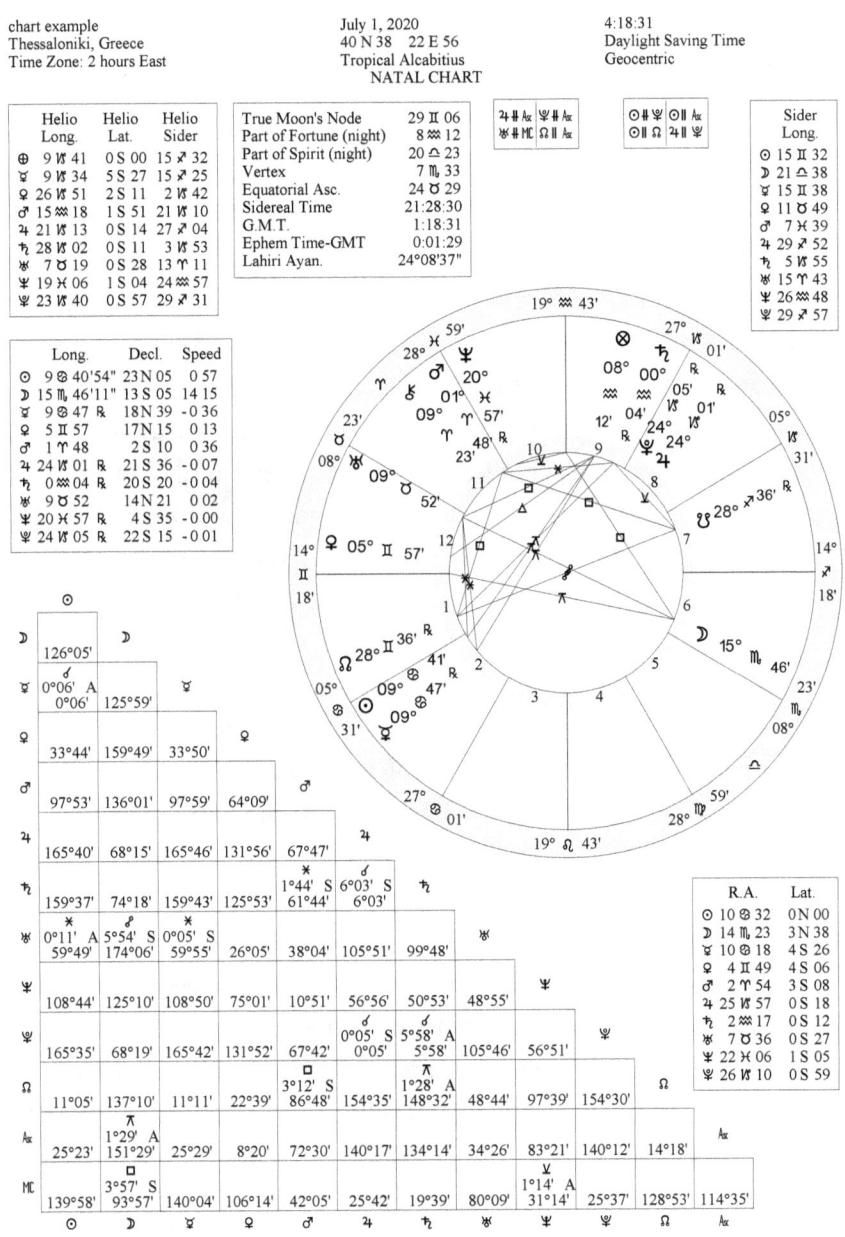

Example Chart 4

in light and moving towards the Sun, which is generally bad. A lot, of course, depends on the actual distance between the Lights.

It is also good when the planet is direct in motion and not appearing from Earth to be moving backwards (retrograde motion). Lilly considered retrograde motion a serious debility. Furthermore, a planet needs to be swift in motion, that is, faster than its average speed. The Sun, Mercury and Venus have an average speed of 1° a day, the Moon of 13½ or so degrees a day, Mars of 32' a day, Jupiter of 5' a day and Saturn of 2' a day. If they are slower than their average speed, this is considered a debility.

In Example Chart 4 on the previous page, Mercury is cazimi, as he is less than 17' (6) away from the Sun. This is cazimi in zodiacal longitude, but not also in latitude, because we see on the bottom right of the page that Mercury's latitude is 4S26 degrees (4° and 26' southern latitude). For some authors, latitude also needs to be less than 17' for this Mercury to be considered cazimi. You also see this R beside Mercury's symbol and this means that he is retrograde, that he moves backwards. The Moon is increasing in light, as she moves further away from the Sun, being a lot faster than he is and still quite some time before becoming Full. Jupiter is still oriental because the Sun is moving away from him, but he will soon become occidental, when the opposition with the Sun becomes exact and the Sun, being much faster than Jupiter, starts moving closer and closer to Jupiter. If we look at the table on the left in the middle, we can see the speeds of the planets. The Sun moves at 0°57' a day, which is his slowest, but one cannot really call the Sun fast or slow, because he has a stable speed. The Moon is quite fast at 14°15' a day, almost one degree more than her average speed, Mercury is retrograde and you can't win or lose points for speed or lack thereof if your motion is retrograde, and the same goes for Jupiter and Saturn. Mars moves at his average speed and Venus is very slow but increasing in speed. We know that, because she is direct and behind the Sun, which means that she will catch up with him at some point and go past him. If she had the same speed but was after the Sun in the zodiac, this would have meant that she was slowing down and would soon be turning retrograde.

A planet's conjunction with the North Node of the Moon is considered to be beneficial for a planet, while the opposite is true for the conjunction with the South Node. The Nodes are the two points where the Moon's orbit intersects with the ecliptic (the Sun's orbit).

A planet is besieged when it's between Mars and Saturn by conjunction or aspect. This is quite bad, unless of course Mars and Saturn are in Capricorn where they have lots of essential dignity.

A planet's conjunction with a fortunate fixed star is something beneficial, while a conjunction with an unfortunate one is considered a debility. The most common fortunate fixed stars are Regulus, Spica, Arcturus, Sirius and Vega, and the most common unfortunate fixed stars are Algol, Scheat, Alcyone and Facies. You can find their current positions on the Internet. You must keep in mind that fixed stars move 1° every 72 years.

Finally, planets rejoice in certain houses. The Sun rejoices in the 9th house, the Moon rejoices in the 3rd house, Mercury rejoices in the 1st, Venus rejoices in the 5th house, Mars rejoices in the 6th house, Jupiter rejoices in the 11th house and Saturn rejoices in the 12th house.

Hayz is also a form of accidental dignity and it refers to sect. There are diurnal and nocturnal charts, as there are diurnal and nocturnal planets. A diurnal chart is one with the Sun above the horizon (the 1st/7th house axis), while a nocturnal chart is one with the Sun below the horizon. Diurnal planets (Jupiter and Saturn) prefer to be in diurnal charts and nocturnal planets (Moon, Mars, Venus) prefer to be in nocturnal charts. Mercury is diurnal when he is oriental and nocturnal when he is occidental. This is quite useful in nativities, in the sense that you can expect more help from your Fortune of sect and less harm from your Infortune of sect. People with diurnal nativities are usually more favoured by Jupiter and less by Venus and can expect more harm from Mars than Saturn. The opposite is true for nocturnal nativities. A diurnal planet is in hayz when it's in a diurnal sign (Aries, Gemini, Leo, Libra, Sagittarius, Aquarius), diurnally placed (where the Sun is), in a diurnal chart. A nocturnal planet is in hayz when it's in a nocturnal sign (Taurus, Cancer, Virgo, Scorpio, Capricorn, Pisces), nocturnally placed (opposite to the place of the Sun), in a nocturnal chart. For some reason, we have an exception for Mars, who is a nocturnal planet, but has to be in a diurnal sign to be in hayz, but I'm not sure I would agree with this. Hayz is particularly important for Venus, because most of the time she is in the same part of the chart as the Sun (the diurnal part) and she is a nocturnal planet, so can only be in hayz when the Sun is in the 1st house and she in the 12th or the Sun in the 6th house and she in the 7th, in a nocturnal sign of course. When this happens it is an extra advantage for Venus because it's not very common, but hayz, in general, is worth being noted for every planet.

And last but not least, the Lot of Fortune is considered a form of accidental dignity when it is in either the house of the querent or the quesited. The Lot of Fortune is calculated by taking the distance from the Sun to the Moon in daytime charts, cast from the ascendant; the distance from the Moon to the Sun is cast from the ascendant in nighttime charts. The LoF is supposed to bring luck and good fortune to the affairs of the house it occupies.

Essential or accidental?

Who wins? Essential dignity or accidental debility? Accidental dignity or essential debility? When both are present, what do we do, if this particular planet is our primary significator? Is our planet in a good state or in a bad state? It depends on the form of dignity or debility. Let's use an essentially dignified Venus and an essentially dignified Moon as our example significators.

a) Essentially dignified Venus vs combustion: Combustion wins, because it's a very serious debility, especially if Venus applies to the Sun. If Venus is separating from the Sun, the combustion is less serious, especially if she is close to getting out of it. Don't make the mistake, though, of treating Venus and Mercury equally. If Mercury is in Virgo, combust, direct and separating from the Sun, this means that he is very fast and probably moves at a speed of 2° degrees a day or more, so the combustion will end pretty soon, but if Venus is 3–4 degrees away from the Sun, it will take her a much longer time to get to an 8-degree distance, because the Sun and Venus are moving practically at the same speed. So a combust Venus, 3–4 degrees separating from the Sun, is still quite serious. However, the essential dignity that Venus has, will make sure that she is not completely destroyed and if we have an applying trine with mutual reception to another planet, then perhaps something can be done, if the Moon also applies to a fortunate aspect.

b) Essentially dignified Venus vs under the beams: Essential dignity wins.

c) Essentially dignified Venus but oriental: No problem at all for Venus.

d) Essentially dignified Venus applying to a square or opposition with Mars or Saturn without a strong mutual reception and the Infortune has no dignity of its own: This is bad. The essential dignity won't help her much.

e) Essentially dignified Venus in a cadent house or in the 6th, 8th or 12th houses: It's a problem, but if Venus makes a fortunate applying aspect with reception, the problem can be overcome.

f) Essentially dignified Venus but retrograde: Again, if she makes an applying aspect with reception, retrogradation is not much of a problem.

g) Essentially dignified Venus conjunct the South Node: It is my opinion that conjunction with the South Node is a very serious debility primarily for the Moon, because it is *her* South Node. For the rest of the planets, it's not something so serious that essential dignity cannot overcome.

h) **Essentially dignified Venus besieged**: This is bad for Venus, unless this happens in Capricorn where both Mars and Saturn are dignified or are at least in Libra where Saturn is in his exaltation and Venus in domicile.

i) **Moon in Cancer decreasing in light**: Provided the Moon is not under the beams, combust or conjunct the South Node, essential dignity wins.

j) **Venus or Moon in Taurus conjunct Algol**: I would go for essential dignity again, although this conjunction must be noted.

Conclusion: Essential dignity is important and can overcome accidental debility in many cases, but combustion and hard aspects to the Infortunes and the Sun without a strong mutual reception are stronger. Pay particular attention to the Moon's conjunction with the South Node.

Accidental dignity vs essential debility

As a rule, accidental dignity almost always wins, except in negligible dignities like swift in motion or direct motion and orientality/occidentality. These dignities won't help a planet in detriment or fall very much. For example, an angular Venus is preferable to Venus in Taurus but in the 12th house or the Moon applying to trine Saturn in Aries (in fall) is preferable to the Moon applying to oppose Saturn in Libra (in exaltation).

Our main job is done. Before we move on to the final step, I just want to say a few words about some minor issues which may prove to be useful in chart interpretation.

a) Natural rulerships: Although our main significators are the house rulers of the querent and the quesited, it can sometimes be useful to also include natural rulers as significators. Here are some basic planetary rulerships:

Saturn: old men, father (in nocturnal charts), teeth, melancholy.

Jupiter: wealth, pregnancy, blood, lungs, liver.

Mars: separation/divorce, surgeon/surgery, male genitals, gallbladder

The Sun: men (in relationship questions), career, heart, brain, right eye in men, left eye in women, father (in diurnal charts).

Venus: love in general (a fortunate aspect between the Moon and Venus is always welcome in a relationship chart), the womb, diabetes, women (in relationship questions), mother (in diurnal charts).

Mercury: astrologers, thieves, learned people, madness, speech impediments.

The Moon: mother (in nocturnal charts), right eye in women, left eye in men, property/land.

Even though there are no outer planets in traditional astrology, Uranus seems to be a disruptive factor in relationship questions, when he is found conjunct the 1st/7th house axis or closely conjunct the Moon. Neptune may be an indication for a new relationship when he is found in the same position as Uranus above and I can't say that I have found any practical use for Pluto, although there may be a connection between Pluto and money or the disease of cancer.

b) Lots: Are the Lots necessary in horary work? Not really, no. If the Lot of Fortune is in the houses of the querent or the quesited, this is a testimony of good fortune, but it's not enough to give us a positive outcome. Here are some other Lots that could also be of use, in cases where the situation is not very clear with our main significators:

Lot of Money/Property: Distance between the ruler of the second house to the cusp of the second house and cast from the ascendant.

Lot of Marriage (men): Distance between Saturn to Venus and cast from the ascendant.

Lot of Marriage (women): Distance between Venus to Saturn and cast from the ascendant.

Lot of Children: Distance between Jupiter and Saturn in diurnal charts (between Saturn and Jupiter in nocturnal charts) and cast from the ascendant.

Lot of Siblings: Distance between Saturn and Jupiter for both diurnal and nocturnal charts and cast from the ascendant (some sources reverse the formula for nocturnal births).

Lot of Sickness: Distance between Saturn and Mars in diurnal charts (the formula is reversed for nocturnal charts) and cast from the ascendant.

Lot of Death: Distance between the Moon to the cusp of the 8th house and cast from the degree of Saturn (no reversal).

What you do is find the degree of the Lot, and the domicile ruler or almuten of this degree can also be used as a significator.

c) Antiscia: This is also something that I think is unnecessary and I'm not convinced of their validity or their importance. Each degree is supposed to have two other "shadow" degrees and these degrees can be found in the following manner:

Each degree of Aries has its antiscium degree in Virgo. If there is a planet at 4° Aries, its antiscium is at 26° Virgo (30 – 4 = 26). A planet at 18° Aries has its antiscium at 12° Virgo (30 – 18 = 12). The degree opposite the antiscium degree is the contra-antiscium degree, so a planet at 4° Aries has its antiscium at 26° Virgo and its contra-antiscium at 26° Pisces. These two degrees are treated as alternative placements for the planet at 4° Aries. So if the Moon, for example, makes no applying aspect to 4° Aries where our significator is, but makes an applying aspect to 26° Virgo or 26° Pisces, this is more or less the same thing, or so they say. I rarely use antiscia in my work. The connections are as follows:

Aries = Virgo/Pisces
Taurus = Leo/Aquarius
Gemini = Cancer/Capricorn
Cancer = Gemini/Sagittarius
Leo = Taurus/Scorpio
Virgo = Aries/Libra
Libra = Pisces/Virgo
Scorpio = Aquarius/Leo
Sagittarius = Capricorn/Cancer
Capricorn = Sagittarius/Gemini
Aquarius = Scorpio/Taurus
Pisces = Libra/Aries

d) The Nodes: To put it in a nutshell, North Node is good, South Node is bad. If they are found in houses we are interested in, then this is either a good or a bad testimony. Also, a conjunction with the South Node can be harmful, especially for the Moon.

e) Signs: Besides diurnal and nocturnal and regardless of their element, signs are also divided into three other categories. Aries, Cancer, Libra and Capricorn are moveable/cardinal signs which show impulsiveness and quick reactions; Taurus, Leo, Scorpio and Aquarius are fixed signs which show stability and a fear of change; and finally, Gemini, Virgo, Sagittarius and Pisces are common/mutable signs which are prone to diversity and a willingness for change. Something that might also be useful in questions about children is whether a sign is fertile or barren. Virgo, Leo and Gemini (although it could show twins) are considered barren and the three water signs (Cancer, Scorpio, Pisces) are the fertile ones. The rest of the signs are indifferent. Finally, as far as temperament goes, fire signs are hot and dry, air signs are hot and moist, earth signs are cold and dry, and water signs are cold and moist.

f) Timing: What we usually do is count the degrees of the applying aspect that shows the outcome and turn that into actual time. If the applying planet needs to travel four degrees to perfect the aspect, then the event will occur in 4 time units, ranging from minutes to years, athough years and minutes rarely make sense in most horary questions. If the aspect is mutually applying, meaning that one planet is retrograde, then things happen sooner. If the Moon is the applying planet, a lot about timing can depend on her speed. A slow Moon may indicate that the event will happen later than expected, while a faster than average Moon is a testimony for the opposite. If the planets are in moveable signs, things happen faster, while in fixed signs, things happen slower. The common signs are somewhere in between. The houses can also play a part in timing. The weaker the houses where the aspect happens, the greater the time unit. I would suggest that you avoid making a choice in most cases, because you can't really say if something will happen in days, weeks or months. Some options can be excluded by logic. Usually, one offers the client the two most logical time units relative to the question asked.

g) About prohibition, frustration etc.: Don't worry about these unnecessary notions. What matters is that the significators of the querent and quesited are brought together. If a third planet intervenes, we need to examine whether this planet is capable of hindering the aspect between our significators. Trines and sextiles can hardly prevent anything, even with the Infortunes. One needs to worry with conjunctions, squares and oppositions without strong receptions. Oppositions will almost always hinder the aspect, unless the opposing planet is a Fortune and there is a strong mutual reception. Conjunctions and squares are not a problem when there is a strong mutual reception between domicile or exaltation.

When our significators are not in aspect or are separating from an aspect, then a third planet can connect the two with a translation or a collection of light. We have a translation of light when a third faster planet is

Step Three – Assessing the Significators

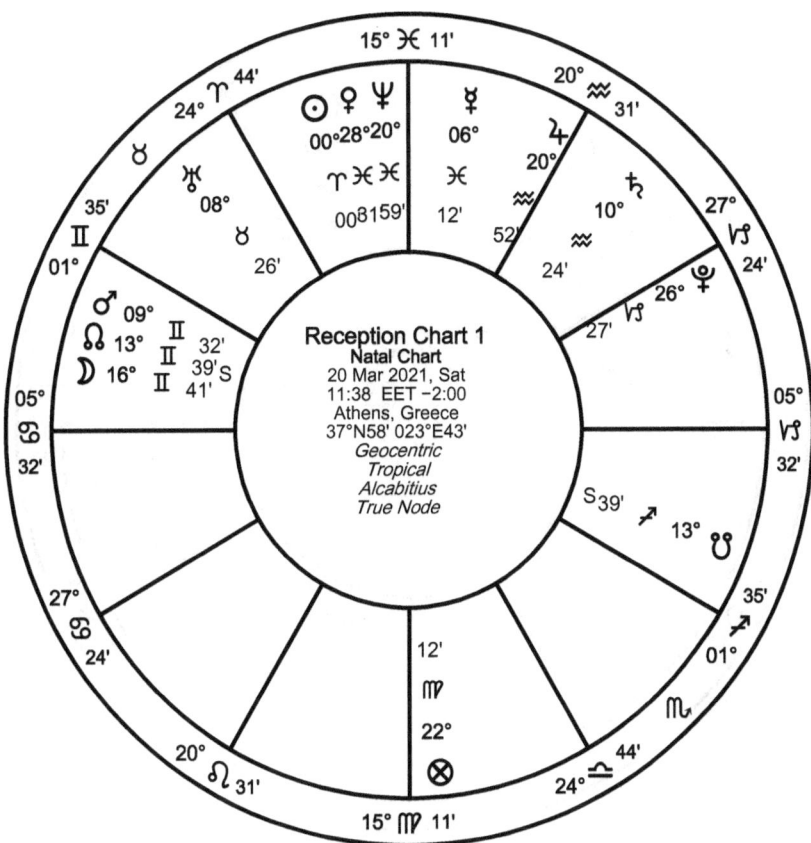

separating from one of our significators and is applying to the other. A collection of light occurs when both our significators apply to a third slower planet who collects their light. In both cases, our two significators must NOT be able to form an aspect on their own, otherwise the third planet is considered an intervention for good or for ill.

In Reception Chart 1, let's say that Jupiter and Saturn are our main significators and we want to bring them together. We see that Jupiter is in the same sign as Saturn, but Jupiter is separating. However, we have the Moon in Gemini separating from Saturn (her last aspect) and applying to Jupiter (her next aspect) and she is therefore connecting them. I must say, though, that in this case we don't need the translation

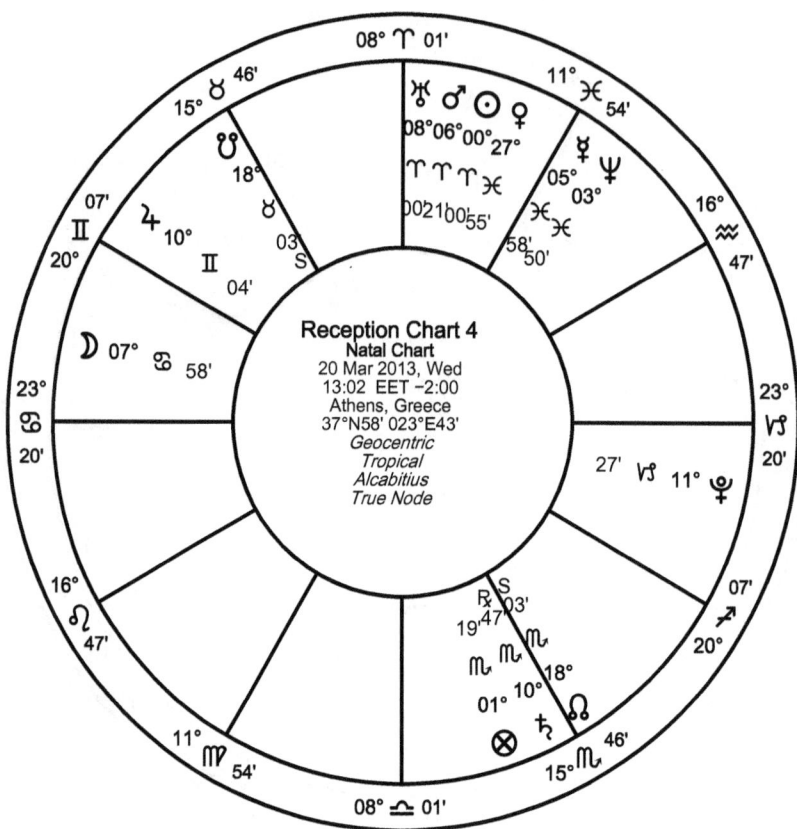

of light. The fact that the Moon, co-significator of all things in a horary chart, is applying to Jupiter with a trine is more than enough.

In Reception Chart 4, let's say that we want to join the Moon and Mercury. The Moon is separating from Mercury, but they both apply to a trine with Saturn and therefore Saturn collects their light.

Translation and collection of light do not work all the time. A lot depends on the nature of the aspects and the presence or lack of receptions.

Final Step

Chart Judgement

As I said before, we are looking for a YES or NO answer. Horary astrologers are not script writers and we do not make up plots. We simply aim to provide an affirmative or a negative answer. Before I start explaining how I suggest judgement be executed, I need to stress one more time one thing that is forgotten by lots of people and is responsible for many mistakes in judgement. Just because Mars and Saturn are significators, this doesn't mean that they stop being Infortunes, which in turn means that if we have an applying square, opposition or conjunction between our two significators and one of them is an Infortune, it would take a very strong mutual reception to get a YES out of it, whereas if the significators are Fortunes, a single reception may suffice. You must not forget as well that the Sun behaves like an Infortune most of the time. Squares and oppositions with the Sun also need strong mutual receptions for a positive outcome and of course the Sun burns the planets close to him by conjunction and this doesn't change when the Sun is a significator.

Finally, keep in mind that planets inside the house of the querent and the quesited do not only act as co-significators, but can also affect these houses for good or for ill. The Fortunes (Venus and Jupiter) are usually a great help, while the Infortunes usually bring misfortune, unless they are essentially dignified and/or well received.

1) The very first thing to do is look at the Moon, the most important planetary body in horary work. Is the Moon applying with a hard aspect (opposition, square, conjunction) to an Infortune (Mars, Saturn) or the Sun without a strong mutual reception (between domicile or exaltation) and they both lack strong essential dignity? Then you need to look no further. The answer to your question, whatever that may be, is NO, even if the Infortune is a significator. The same, more or less, applies to the ruler of the ascendant, although the Moon's testimony is more powerful. For example, if the Moon in Gemini applies to an opposition with Saturn in Sagittarius (no strong mutual reception and no dignity for Saturn), then the outcome cannot be positive for the querent. If Saturn is in a strong mutual reception with Jupiter in Libra, then he is not that much of an Infortune and the rest of the chart needs to be checked, although the opposition the Moon makes to Saturn remains a problem. If both the Moon and the Infortune are very strong essentially (e.g. the Moon in Cancer and Saturn in Capricorn), then something can come out of this, particularly if there is a third planet that sextiles/trines the Moon and Saturn and there are receptions. Finally, if the Moon is in Cancer or Taurus (very strong) and applies to conjunct an Infortune, this does not necessarily prevent a positive outcome, because the Infortune in this case is completely surrendered to the power of the Moon by being in the same sign as her. If it were a square or an opposition, things would have been different.

Final Step – Chart Judgement

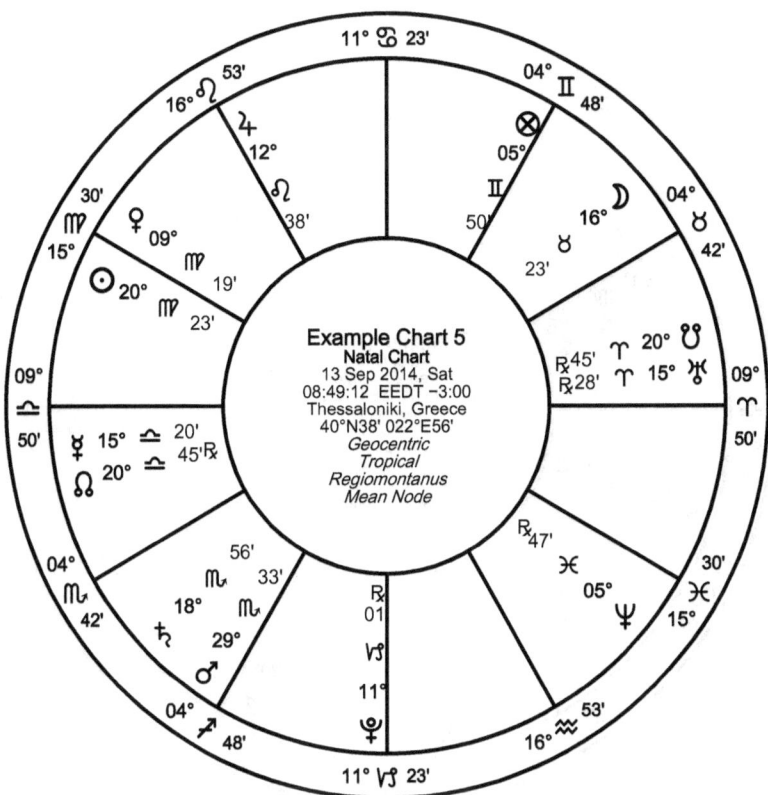

In Example Chart 5, the Moon is applying to oppose Saturn. The Moon is exalted and there is a mutual reception between Saturn and Mars (domicile/terms). There is even a third planet (the Sun) that trines the Moon and sextiles Saturn. However, there is no strong reception between the two opposing planets and the houses of the Moon, Saturn and the Sun are three of the worst houses in a chart. This opposition cannot be saved. The answer to the question, whatever that may be, is NO.

In Example Chart 6, there is also a Moon/Saturn opposition. However, the opposition is in better houses than before, even though cadent. Saturn has dignity by terms and face and has a very strong mutual reception with Jupiter in the 1st house of the querent (domicile,

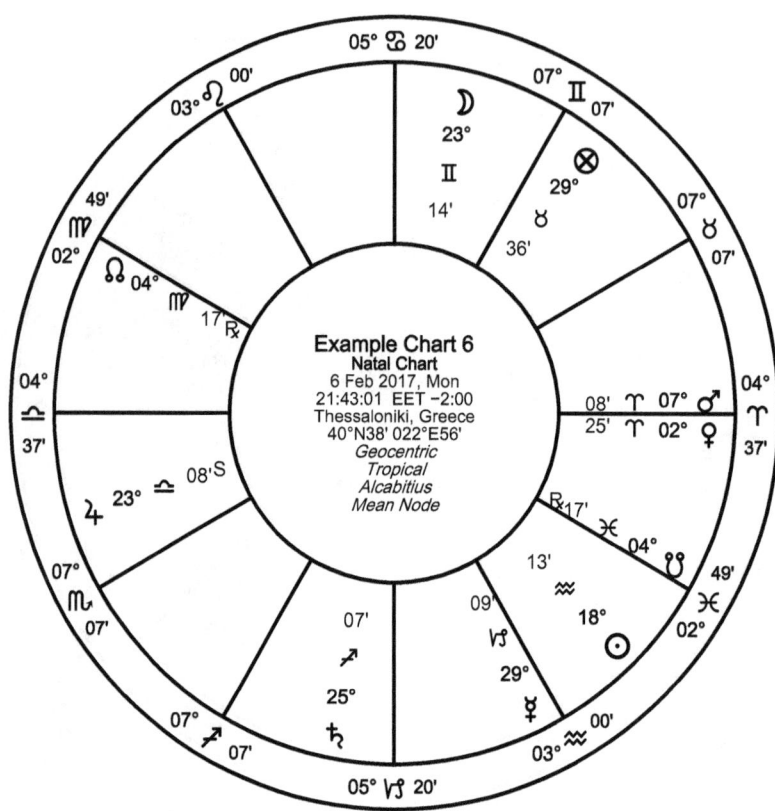

triplicity/exaltation); the Moon forms a partile trine with Jupiter and Jupiter sextiles Saturn; the Sun sextiles/trines Saturn and the Moon, who has a mutual reception with Mercury (domicile/triplicity). This opposition is saved, mainly because of the very strong mutual reception between Jupiter and Saturn and Jupiter's presence in the 1st house of the querent. The answer in this case is not a definite NO and the rest of the testimonies need to be examined in detail before a conclusion is reached. However, one can still expect some problems because of the opposition.

In Example Chart 7, we have again a Moon/Saturn opposition. However, they are both very strong essentially (they are both in domicile) and Saturn has also a very strong mutual reception with Mars (domicile/

Final Step – Chart Judgement

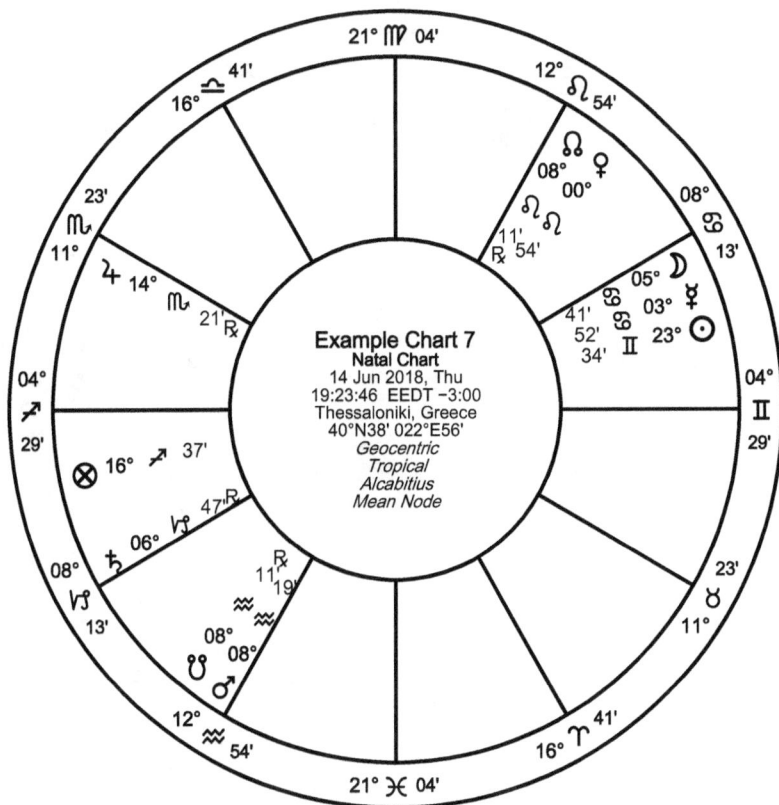

exaltation), but no aspect between them. Jupiter, a Fortune, trines and sextiles the Moon/Saturn opposition (the aspects are not close, though) and there is reception (Jupiter receives the Moon in his exaltation and Saturn is in Jupiter's face) although not anything impressive. One may proceed, but with extreme caution.

Now, if the ruler of the ascendant paints a completely different picture from the Moon, it's sometimes best to refrain from giving judgement, although I have to say that the Moon usually takes precedence because it is the Moon that shows mainly the flow of events. So if the ruler of the ascendant applies to a trine with the ruler of the quesited (fortunate testimony), but the Moon applies to an opposition with Saturn without reception, it is the Moon that will usually prevail. However, the fortunate testimonies may stand and show that every cloud has a silver lining.

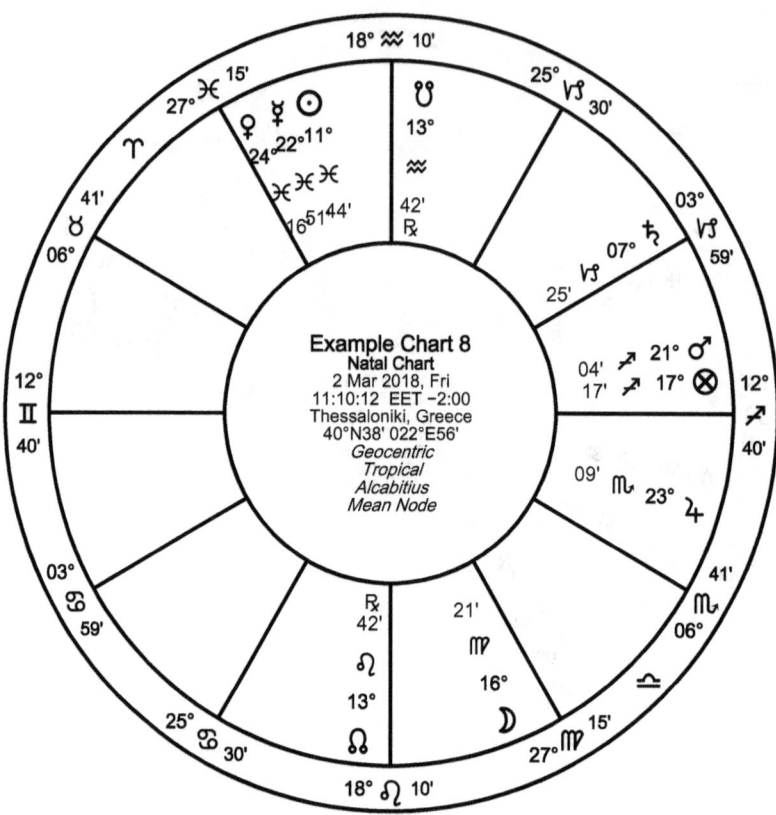

Example Chart 8 is a question about a possible pregnancy. Normally, I would consider the chart invalid, because of Mars in the 7th (the astrologer), but here Mars is in a very strong mutual reception with Jupiter. In both the Regiomontanus and Alcabitius house systems, Libra is intercepted in the 5th house, so the baby is signified by both Mercury (Virgo on the cusp of the 5th house) and Venus (domicile ruler of the intercepted sign in the 5th house). Mercury also signifies the querent (Gemini on the ascendant). Mercury is applying to trine Jupiter, the natural ruler of pregnancy, and after that he will conjunct a very strong Venus (significator of the baby) in extremely fertile Pisces. Judging by this testimony alone, the querent must be pregnant. The Moon, however, applies to square an Infortune, Mars, without a strong mutual reception and this is very negative (the Moon also opposes the

Sun, Mercury and Venus, and Mars afflicts Mercury and Venus). The querent wasn't pregnant. The Moon is severely afflicted (separates from an opposition to the Sun and applies to a square with Mars) and this completely overrides any fortunate testimonies.

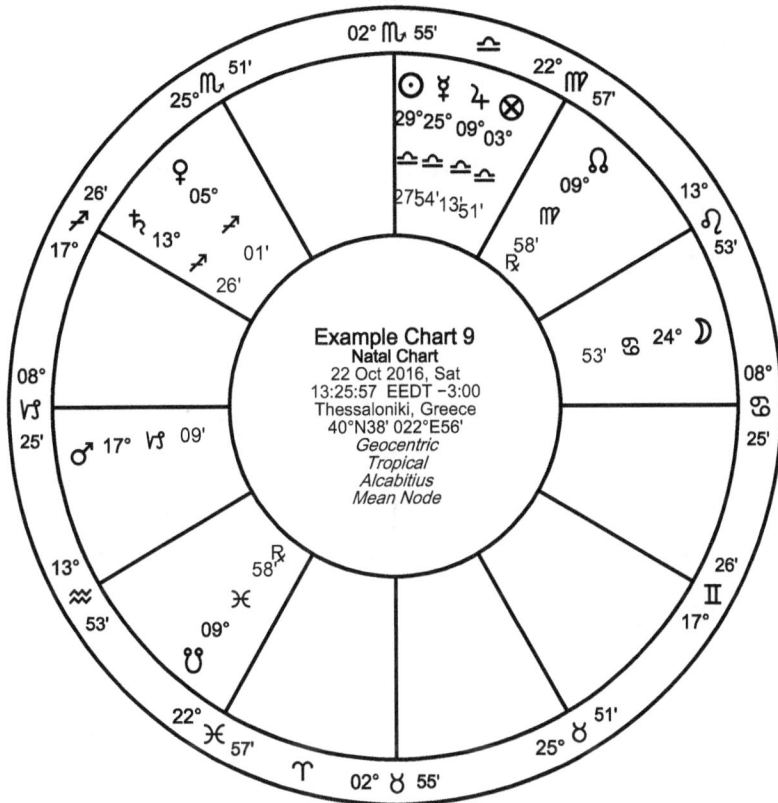

Example Chart 9 was a question about buying a house. The Moon applies to a square with Mercury and then to a square with the Sun. The square with Mercury is not really something to worry about, because Mercury is not an Infortune and the Moon is particularly strong, angular and in her domicile and face. The square with the Sun could be a problem, though, despite the Moon's great essential and accidental strength, but it's not an automatic NO, because the Moon is very strong essentially and accidentally and the Sun has a mutual reception with Venus (domicile/triplicity) and Saturn (exaltation/triplicity). We need, therefore, to see what the other significators are doing. Venus is the significator of the house for sale (4th house domicile ruler), but she is also the almuten of the 7th house, which signifies the seller. Venus is in a very strong mutual reception with Jupiter, and Saturn, the significator of the querent, is also in a very strong mutual reception with Jupiter. Venus is applying to conjunct Saturn, who behaves very well here because of his mutual reception with Jupiter. Mars, a 1st house significator, is also strongly dignified by being angular and in his exaltation and face. The querent bought the house. In this chart, the negative testimony of the Moon was overridden by her own dignity and the great strength of the various mutual receptions.

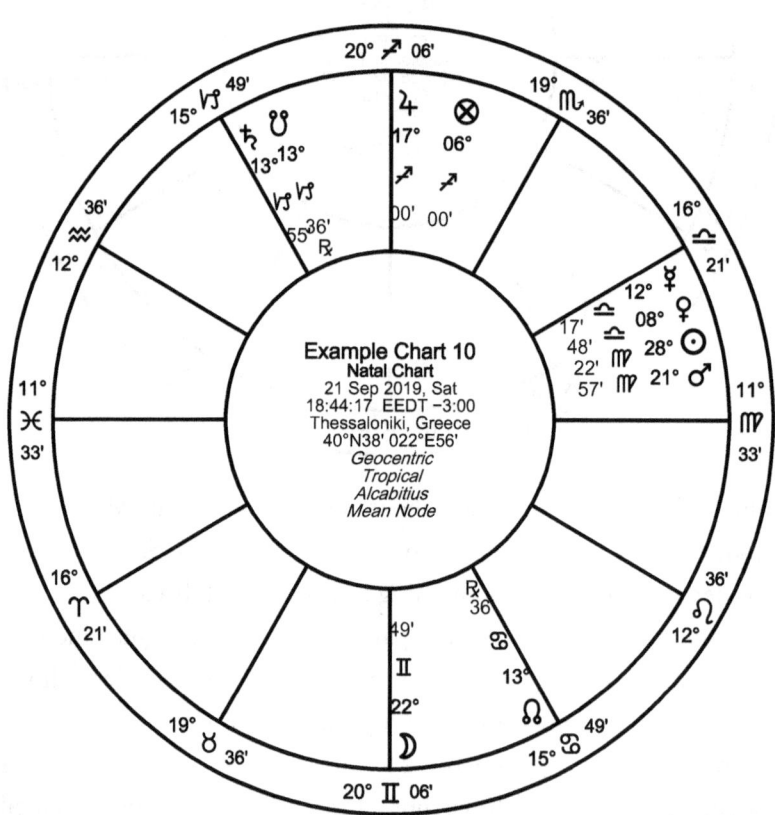

Example Chart 10 was a question about a possibly stolen car. We see the car, Mars, combust in the 7th house of thieves, so we can confirm the car was stolen. The car is treated here as a 2nd house possession, because that's what the querent was interested in. We then see the Moon separating from a square to Mars and applying to a square to the Sun. We can say the Moon is besieged, because the Sun behaves like an Infortune to the planet who aspects it with a hard aspect without a strong mutual reception. So nothing good can come out of this. And so it proved. The car was never found. However, the domicile ruler of the ascendant, Jupiter, is extremely strong conjunct the MC and in his other domicile, and the almuten of the ascendant, Venus, is also very strong in Libra in the 8th house of other people's money. These testimonies show the querent in a very good condition and contradict the negative testimony of the Moon. The testimony of the Moon may have prevailed, but, as it turned out, something good came out of it all. The querent, mostly with the money he received from the insurance company, bought a used car that he now says is much better than the stolen one.

2) If neither the Moon nor the ruler of the ascendant make an *applying* aspect to the ruler of the quesited in the signs they all are, this doesn't mean NO necessarily, but a lot will depend on the next aspect they both will make. Is it a trine or a sextile with reception? Is it a conjunction with a Fortune or any other planet (except for the Sun), with a strong reception? If this is the case for both, or one of them and the other significator is problem-free, then the answer is probably YES, regardless of the fact that there is no connection between querent and quesited. If the aspect is a square or an opposition with no strong mutual reception, then the answer is probably NO.

Example Chart 11 is about a lawsuit (no adversary, the querent wanted a certain law to be applied in her own case as well). Mars may be in the 7th house (consideration before judgement), but he is in a strong mutual reception with Jupiter, so we can proceed. The ruler of the ascendant, Mercury, applies to conjunct a strongly dignified Venus in Pisces and the Moon applies to a sextile with Mars. Both these aspects are positive (no reception between the Moon and Mars, but the conjunction between Mercury and Venus seems enough) and the answer is YES. We don't need to go looking for dubious significators of the quesited. Both our main significators are problem-free.

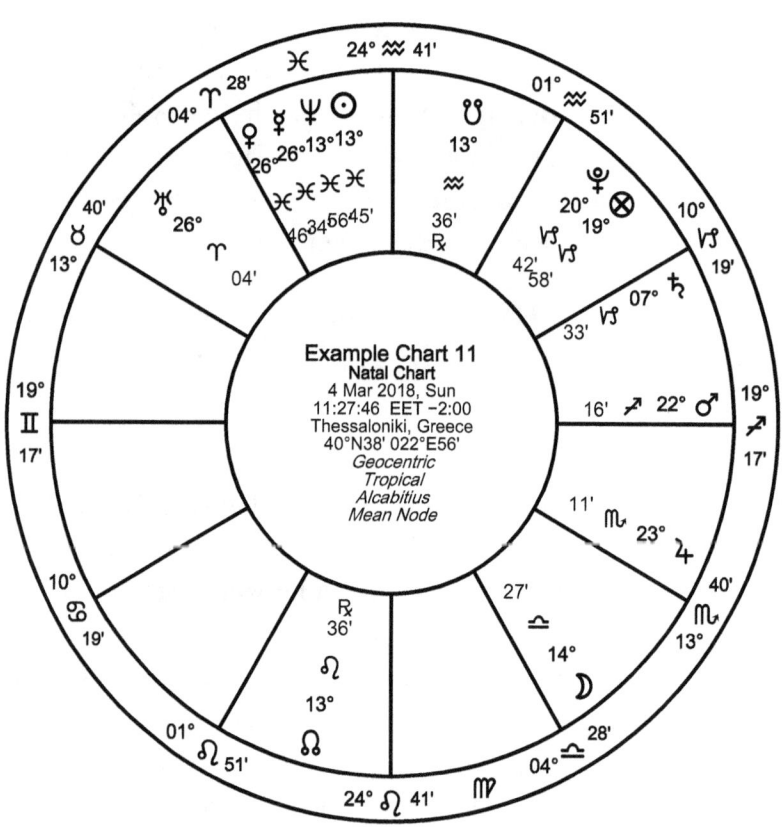

Final Step – Chart Judgement

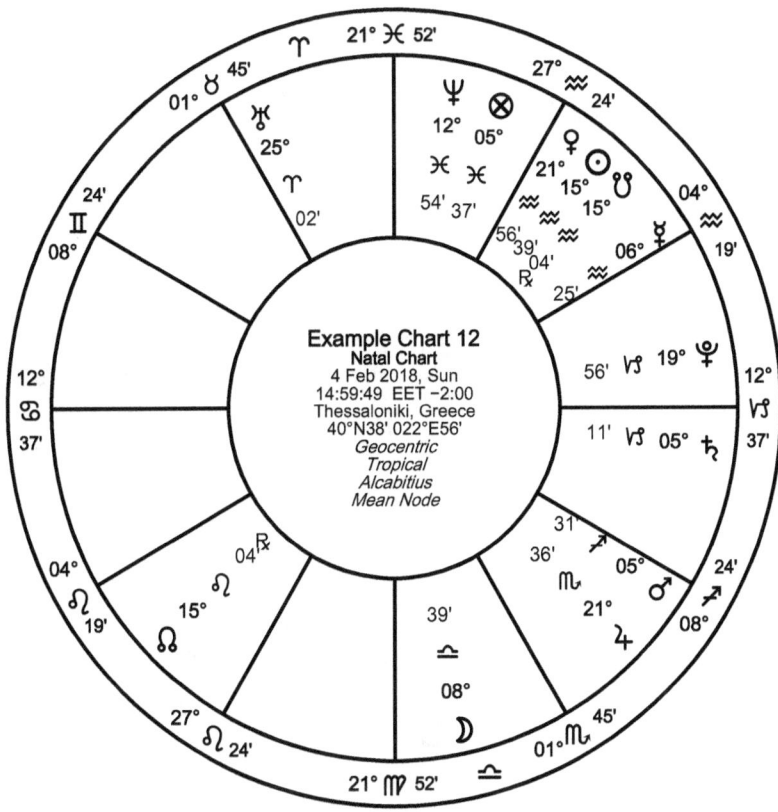

Example Chart 12 was a relationship question. The significators of the querent are the Moon, domicile ruler of the ascendant, and Venus, co-almuten of the ascendant. The significators of the quesited are Saturn and Mars (co-almuten). The Moon has separated from both Saturn and Mars, while Venus makes no aspect with either of them. The Moon though, applies to a trine with the Sun and Venus. Trines are usually enough to give a YES, but in this case the Sun and Venus are in a dreadful state. The Sun is in detriment, in the 8th house, and exactly conjunct the South Node, while Venus is also in the 8th house and combust. These trines cannot produce a fortunate outcome and combined with Saturn in the 7th house (in relationship questions, when the ruler of the 7th house is in the 7th house, this usually indicates that the other person is not interested), the answer was NO.

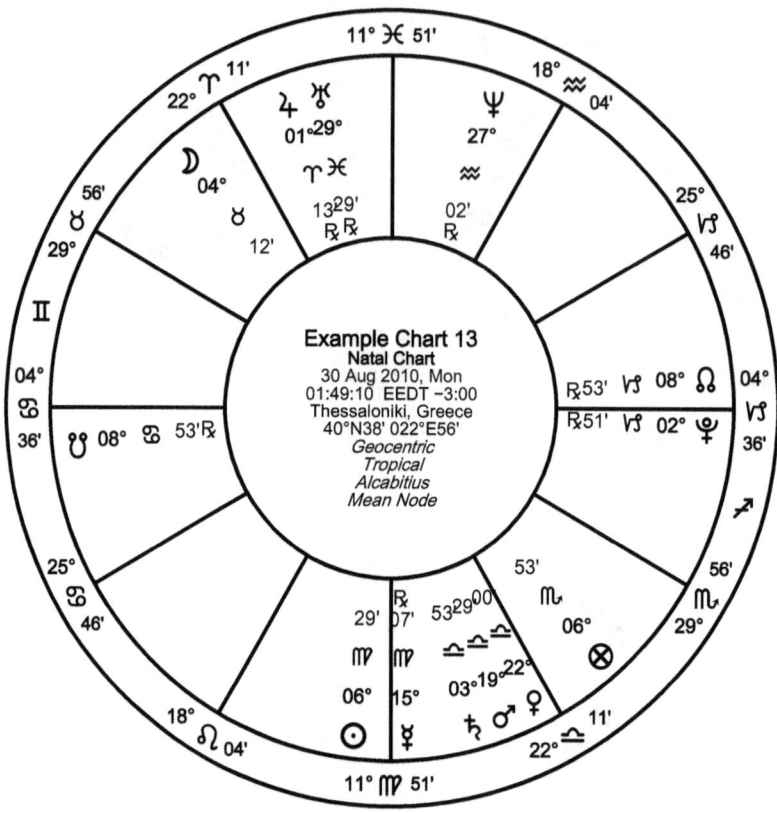

Example Chart 13 was a sports question. The significators of the team are the Moon and Mars (co-almuten) and the significators of the win are Jupiter (domicile ruler) and Venus (co-almuten). The Moon doesn't make any aspect with either Jupiter or Venus, but she makes a fortunate trine with the Sun with reception. That's good, but since there is no aspect, good or bad, with the significators of the win, we need to check what Mars is doing. Mars is in detriment and Venus, one significator of the win, even though slow, she is still faster than him and the conjunction won't happen in Libra. Both Saturn and Venus though, receive him. Mars will not make an aspect with Jupiter either. What about the win itself? Venus is slow, afflicted by Mars, but in her own domicile which means that Mars surrenders to her, and Jupiter is in his triplicity and terms, but retrograde and opposed by Saturn, although

Jupiter is separating and Saturn is not a true malefic in this chart. These are testimonies that show promise, but cannot entirely guarantee the win. Perhaps we should bring in the adversary, although this is not necessary in most cases and it's best if we leave them out, but in this case we lack certainty. The opponent is signified by Saturn in exaltation and in a very strong mutual reception with Venus, while they have the North Node inside their house and our team is afflicted by the South Node. The opponent won.

⋘⋙

3) If the ruler of the ascendant or the Moon make an applying aspect to the ruler of the quesited, but it's NOT the next aspect they both make, we need to see whether the aspect that intervenes hinders the aspect with the ruler of the quesited. If the intervening aspect is a trine or sextile, with or without reception, there can be no hindrance. If the aspect is a square with a strong mutual reception between domicile or exaltation, hindrance is doubtful. The matter is hindered when the next aspect is a square without a strong mutual reception or an opposition. If the planet who intervenes does so by conjunction, there is no problem if the planet is a Fortune or any other planet in domicile or exaltation who receives our significator. If there is no reception and the planet is an Infortune or the Sun, the matter is hindered. Finally, if our significator is itself in domicile or exaltation, then the intervening planet by conjunction is under the significators' power, so hindrance is doubtful.

Here is Example Chart 4 again. It's a relationship question and we see the Moon applying to the almuten of the 7th house and natural ruler of men, the Sun. However, like I said before, the Moon's next aspect is not the trine to the Sun, but the opposition to Saturn, which can't be saved. The trine is hindered and the answer is NO. Uranus in the 7th house making an exact opposition to Mercury in the 1st doesn't help either, neither does the South Node also in the 7th house.

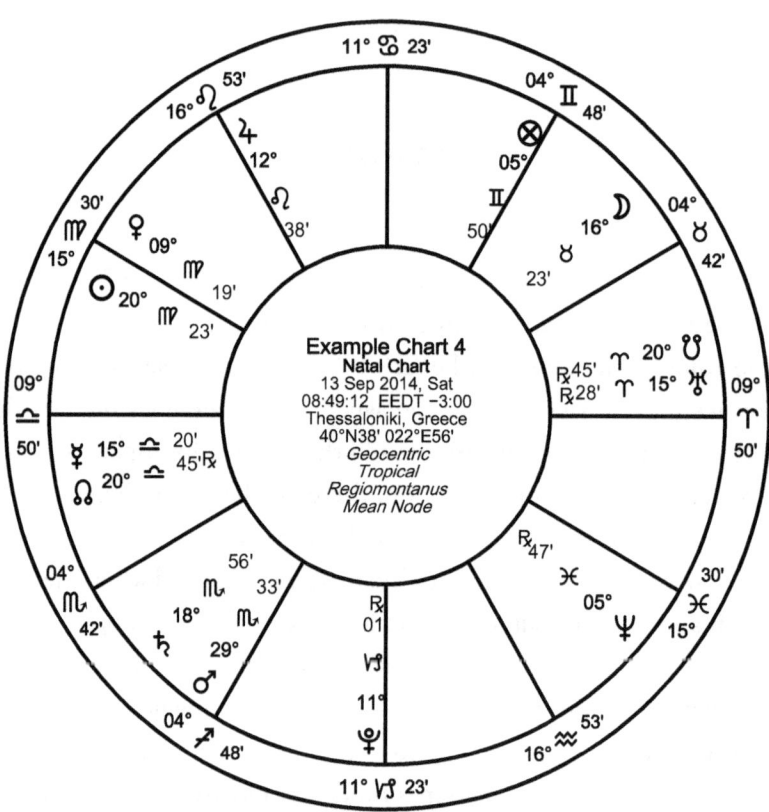

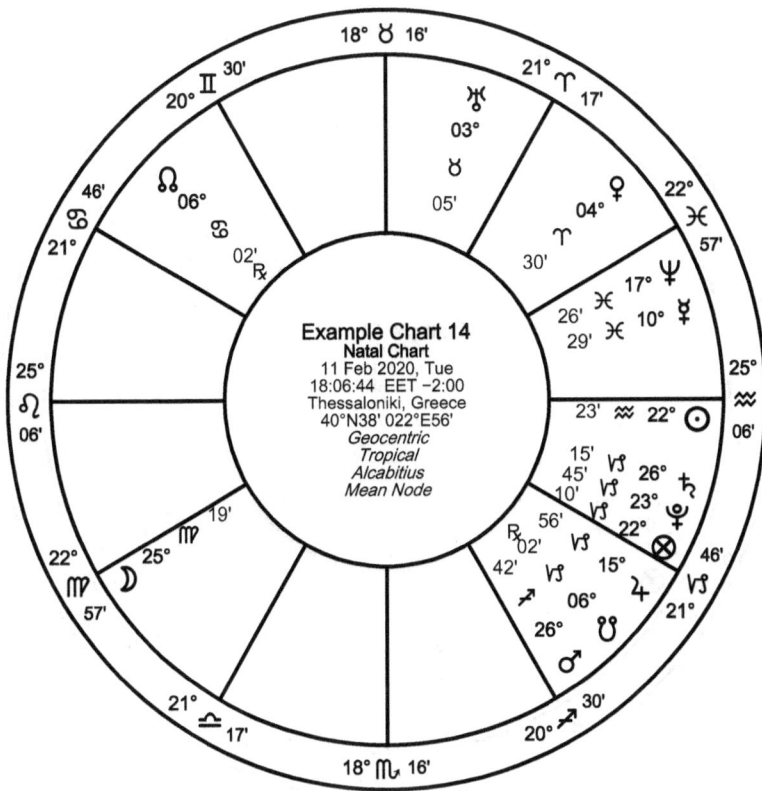

In Example Chart 14, the querent would like to go to a concert, but she is afraid it won't take place. The concert is better signified by Mars, who is in the 5th house of entertainment and is the ruler of the 9th house (the concert was in a foreign country). The Sun (ascendant ruler) won't sextile Mars (they have to both change signs before this can happen) and the Moon's next aspect is a trine to Saturn. Trines cannot hinder anything, so the square of the Moon to Mars is safe. Nonetheless, we are talking about a square with an Infortune without a strong mutual reception, and Mars afflicts the 5th house by his presence there. Jupiter, the ruler of the 5th house, is received by Saturn, but he is in fall and in the 6th house with no applying fortunate aspects. The answer is NO.

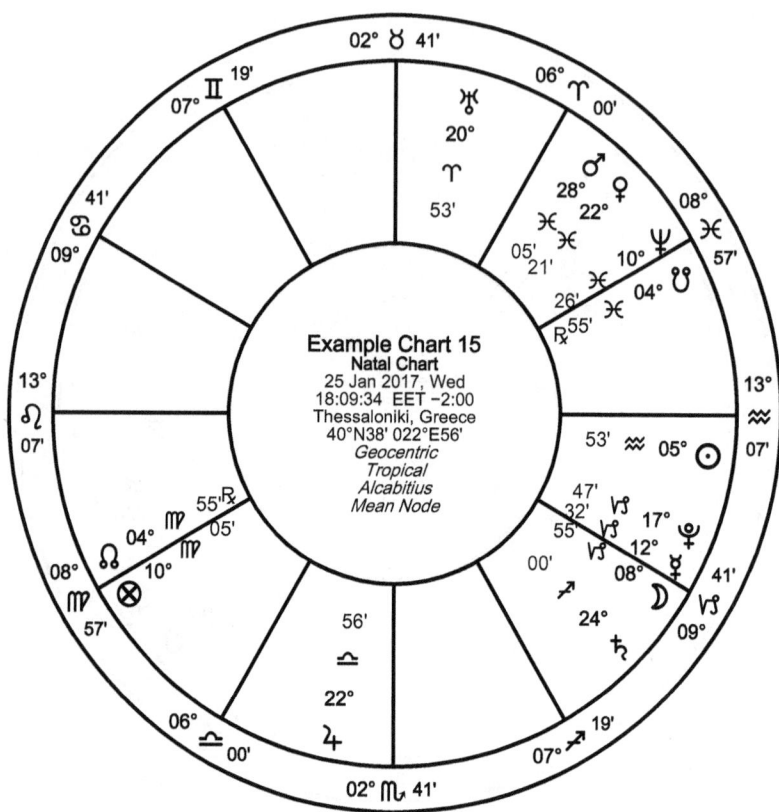

Example Chart 15 was a sports question. The Moon applies to sextile Venus, the significator of the win, but Venus is not the Moon's next aspect. If it were, the chart would have been invalid anyway, because the aspect is out of orb and I consider this Moon void of course. The Moon's next aspect is Mercury, who is not an Infortune and he is in a mutual reception with Jupiter in Libra (triplicity/terms). This conjunction, therefore, is not a hindrance and the sextile from the Moon to Venus stands. Venus appears afflicted by Saturn, but Saturn has this wonderful mutual reception with Jupiter in Libra and he is not a big problem, while she has her own wonderful mutual reception with Jupiter. Mars is not a problem either, not only because Venus is so strong, but also because he is in his triplicity and face. Anyway, the sextile between Venus and the Moon will happen before the square between Venus and Saturn. The answer is YES.

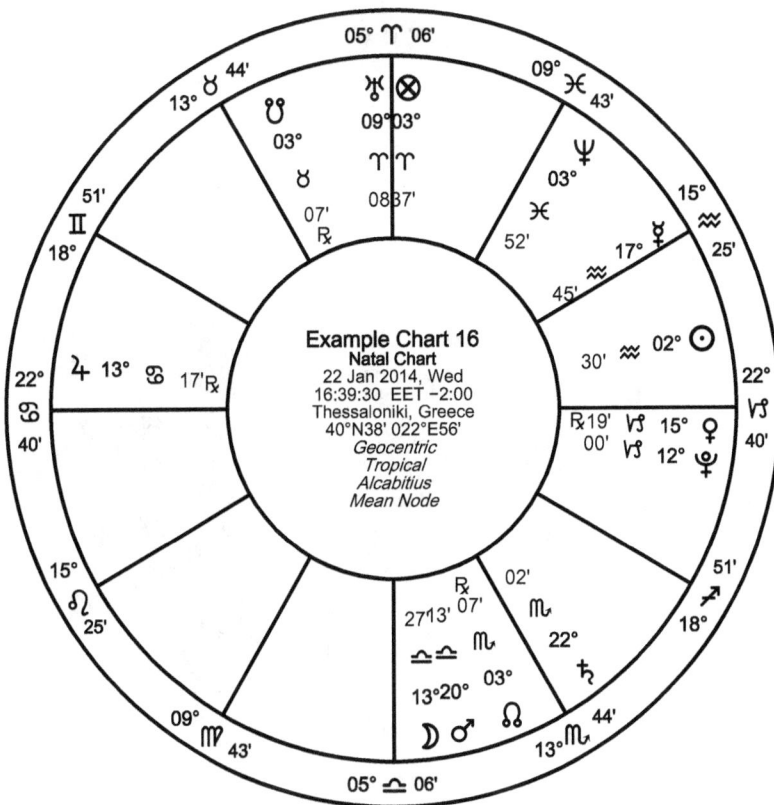

Example Chart 16 was a sports question. The Moon, domicile ruler and co-almuten of the ascendant, makes an applying aspect with Mars, the significator of the win, but before that happens, the Moon first forms a square with Venus and a trine with Mercury. Trines are never a problem and the square wirh Venus is also not a problem here, because Venus is a Fortune, angular and in her triplicity and terms (although retrograde). The conjunction with Mars stands, but to no avail, because it is a conjunction with an Infortune in detriment and there is no strong reception to offset this. The team lost.

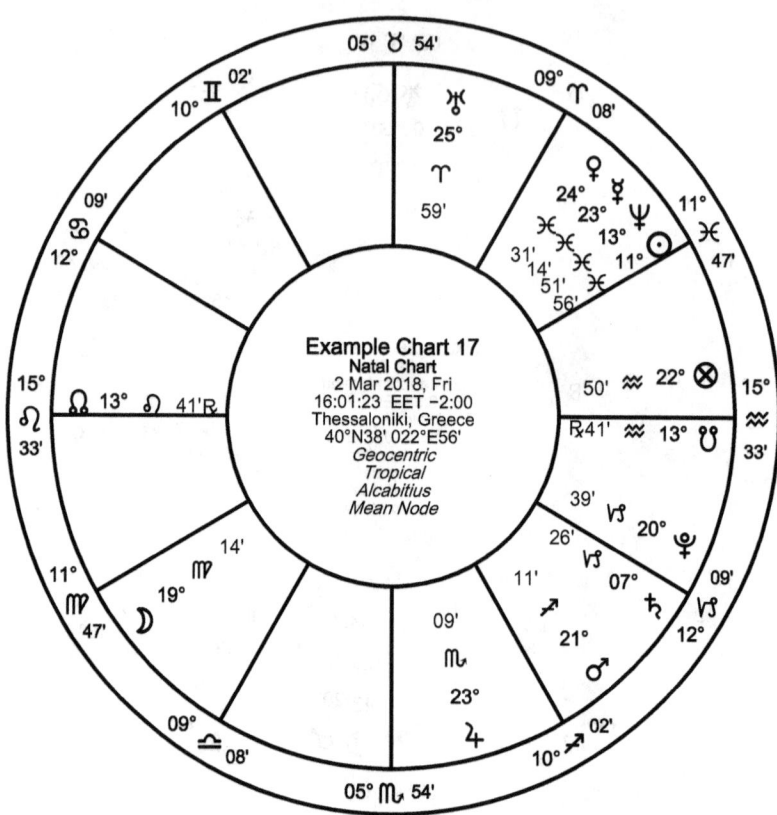

Example Chart 17 was a 10th house question. The Moon will make an opposition with Venus, the significator of the win, and even though it's an opposition, there is Jupiter that trines Venus and sextiles the Moon and Venus is very strong essentially. Can the opposition be saved? We don't care, because the Moon's very next aspect is a square with Mars, an Infortune, and there is no strong mutual reception. Whatever happens next and no matter how positive it can be, it is hindered by this square, which is so negative that we hardly need to check what the 1st house significator is doing. The answer is NO.

4) If the next aspect of the Moon or the ruler of the ascendant is the ruler of the quesited, then we are done. We just need to examine the kind of aspect we are talking about. A trine is the best solution, as no reception is needed. A sextile needs a reception most of the time, unless the planets involved have essential dignity. A square needs a strong mutual reception between domicile or exaltation, if one of the significators is an Infortune or the Sun, or a strong single reception by domicile or exaltation, if one of the significators is a Fortune without much dignity. If the Fortune has sufficient dignity, it is possible that a single reception with a minor dignity (except for face) may be enough. With Mercury, a mutual reception at least between lesser dignities (triplicity and terms) is needed most of the time, unless Mercury is strongly dignified essentially. An opposition can only be saved if there is a strong mutual reception between the significators and a third planet that sextiles/trines with reception the two opposing planets. Even so, there may still be a problem. An applying conjunction with the Sun is combustion and therefore the answer is NO, unless the Sun is in Leo or Aries and strongly receives the combust planet or the combust planet is in its domicile or exaltation. If the combust planet is separating from the Sun and the other main significator (the ruler of the ascendant or the Moon) makes a fortunate next aspect, then a positive outcome may be possible. A conjunction with an Infortune is bad, unless the Infortune is in the sign of its domicile or exaltation and therefore strongly receives the other planet.

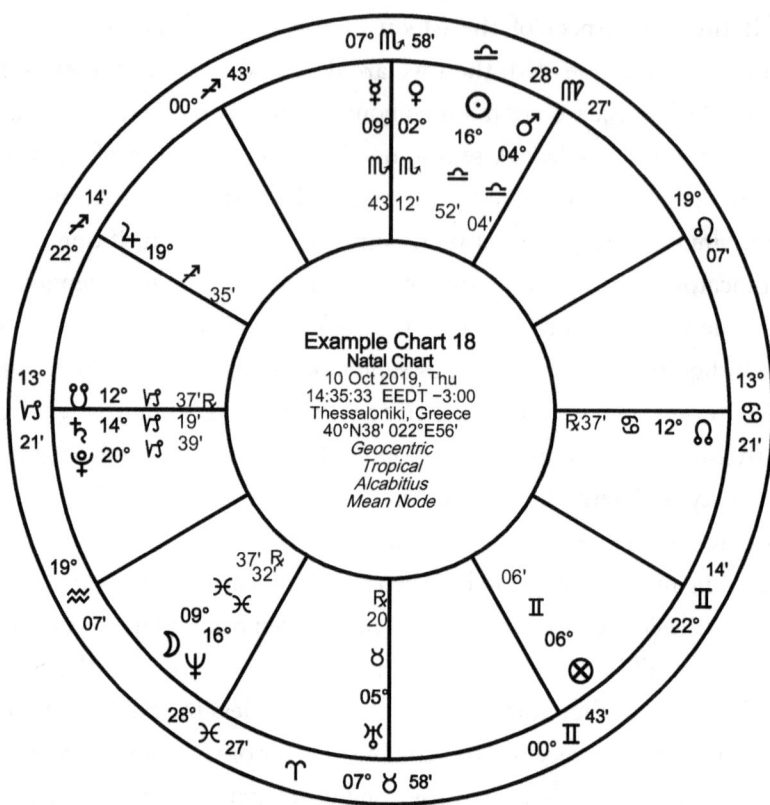

Example Chart 18 was a sports question. The Moon applies with a trine to Mercury, a significator of the win, because he is in the 10th house. This is usually enough, but, to be sure, let's see what else happens in the chart, in case the ruler of the ascendant paints a completely different picture. Mars, co-almuten of the ascendant and domicile ruler/almuten of the 10th house, has left combustion and he is in a strong mutual reception with Venus in her own triplicity conjunct the 10th house cusp. Saturn, domicile ruler of the ascendant, is in the 1st house and in his own domicile, in a strong mutual reception with Mars. The only problem in the chart is the South Node on the ascendant and the square from the Sun to Saturn, but there is reception (Saturn receives the Sun in his exaltation) and the aspect is separating. A fortunate chart on the whole and the answer is YES.

Final Step – Chart Judgement 77

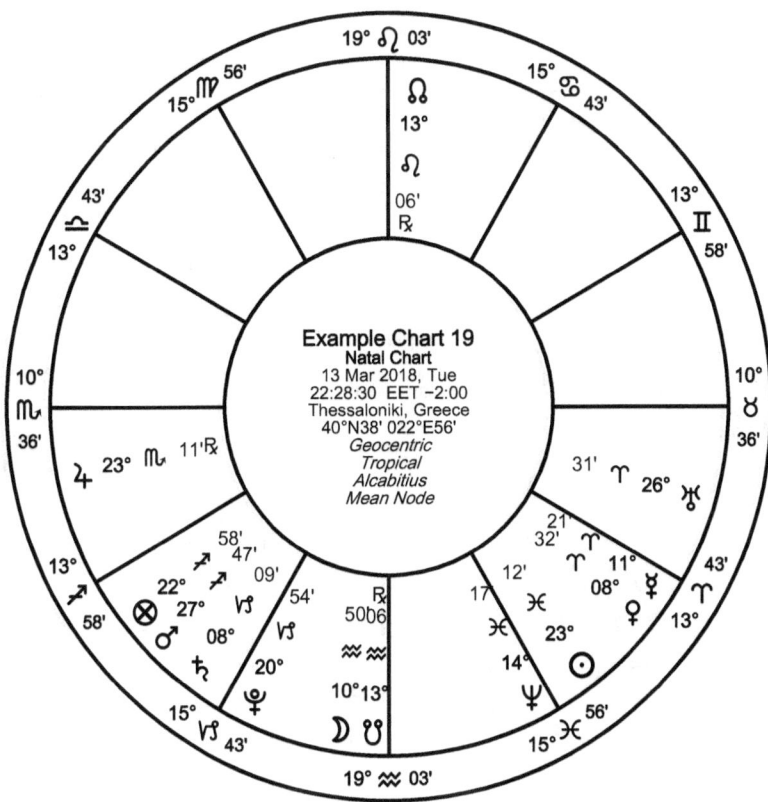

Example Chart 19 was a sports question. The Moon applies to a sextile with Mercury with reception (the Moon is in Mercury's triplicity), but Mercury is not a significator and the Moon is afflicted by her conjunction with the South Node. Like I said before, the conjunction with the South Node may be generally considered bad, but I think this is especially so for the Moon, because it is *her* South Node. So the sextile is certainly not enough in this case. There is a partill (exact) trine with reception between the Sun (10th house domicile ruler) and Jupiter in the 1st house, so he is a significator of the team. This is good, but the aspect is unfortunately separating. The Sun is applying to a square with Mars, but this will happen after they both change signs and even if it happened before, this wouldn't be a good thing. The answer is NO.

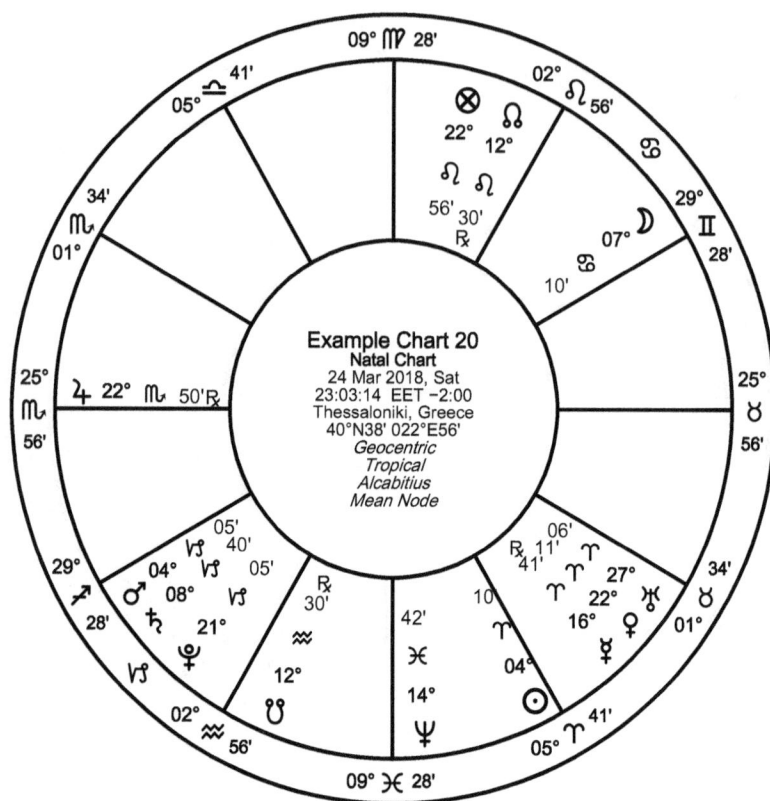

Example Chart 20 was a sports question. The Moon has just separated from a square with the Sun and applies to oppose Saturn. We don't like that, but the Moon is in domicile and the two Infortunes are strongly dignified, so this is not an automatic NO. The Moon, however, applies next (after her opposition with Saturn) to a square with Mercury, the significator of the win, who is retrograde and under the beams moving into combustion. The Sun receives Mercury and Mercury won't be completely destroyed by the combustion, but still, we are talking about a square with a weak retrograde planet without reception. Mars, domicile ruler and almuten of the ascendant, is essentially strong, but he is afflicted by the exact square with the Sun and Jupiter on the ascendant is certainly not enough to give us a positive outcome. The team lost.

Final Step – Chart Judgement

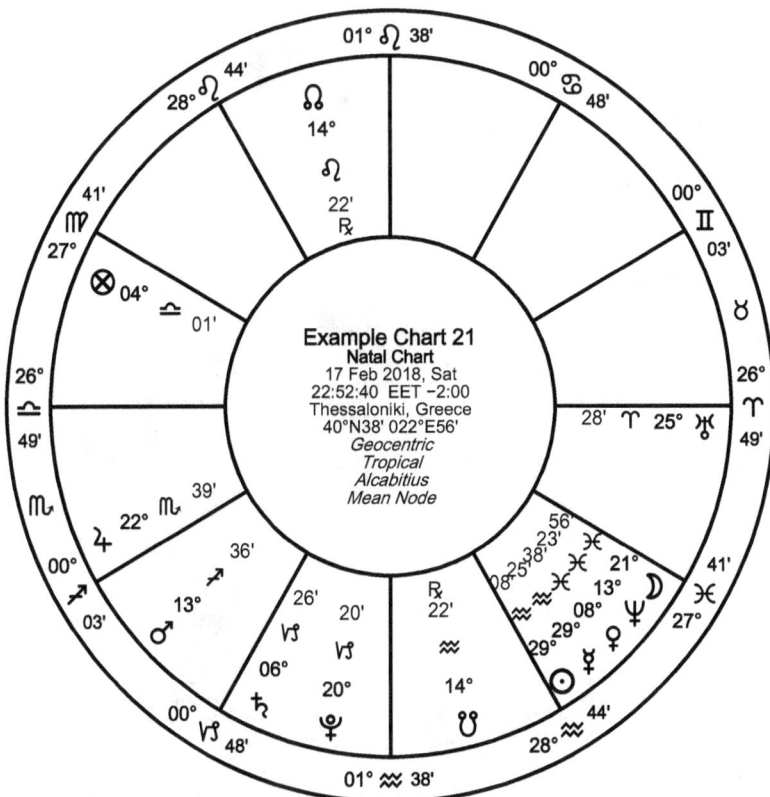

Example Chart 21 was a sports question. The Moon applies to a trine with Jupiter in the 1st house (in the intercepted sign in the 1st house) with a strong single reception. Even if one used the Regiomontanus house system, which places Jupiter in the 2nd house, Jupiter is still the 10th house co-almuten. This should be enough, but because neither the Moon nor Jupiter aspects the ascendant, let's do some more checking. Venus, domicile ruler and almuten of the ascendant, is very strong in Pisces (exaltation and terms), but she applies to a square with Mars, an Infortune and ruler of the intercepted sign in the 1st house. There is a mutual reception, though, between triplicity and terms, which is normally not enough, but Venus is very strong essentially and we also have here the Moon/Jupiter trine. The team won.

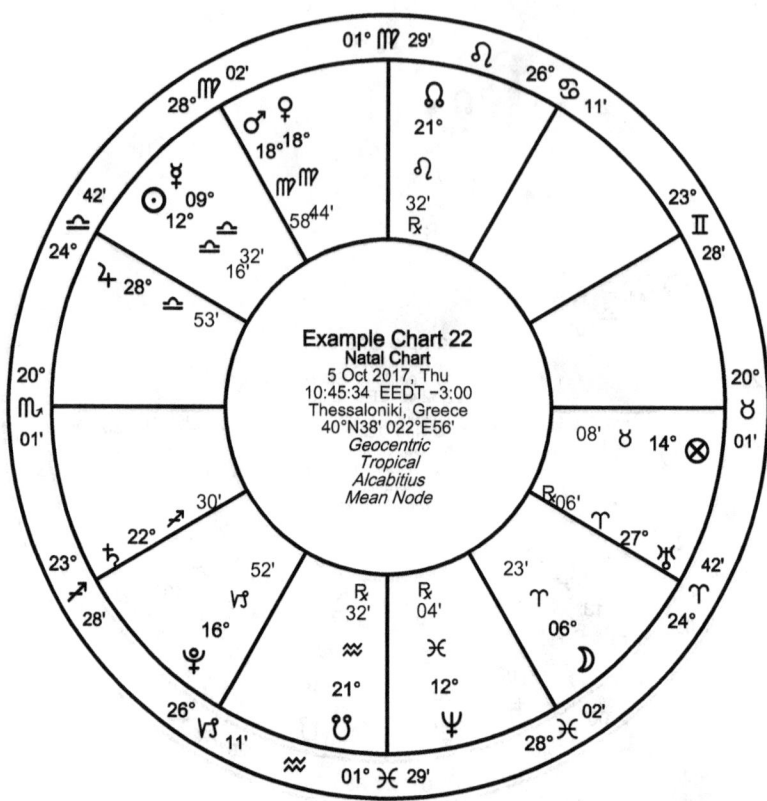

Example Chart 22 was a relationship question. The significator of the querent, Mars, forms a partill conjunction with the significator of the partner, Venus, who is helped by her strong mutual reception with Mercury. Mars, though, is an Infortune and the planet of separation, so contrary to popular belief, this conjunction is not fortunate, because the single reception by triplicity with an Infortune is not enough. This is another example of a very basic rule, that just because an Infortune is a main significator, the Infortune doesn't stop being an Infortune. What's more, both Mars and Venus apply to Saturn, the other Infortune. We've seen this particular Saturn (in Sagittarius, in mutual reception with Jupiter in Libra) behave really well and not like an Infortune, so let's go and see what the Moon is doing. The Moon applies to an opposition with Mercury and the Sun. That's very negative. The answer is most

Final Step – Chart Judgement

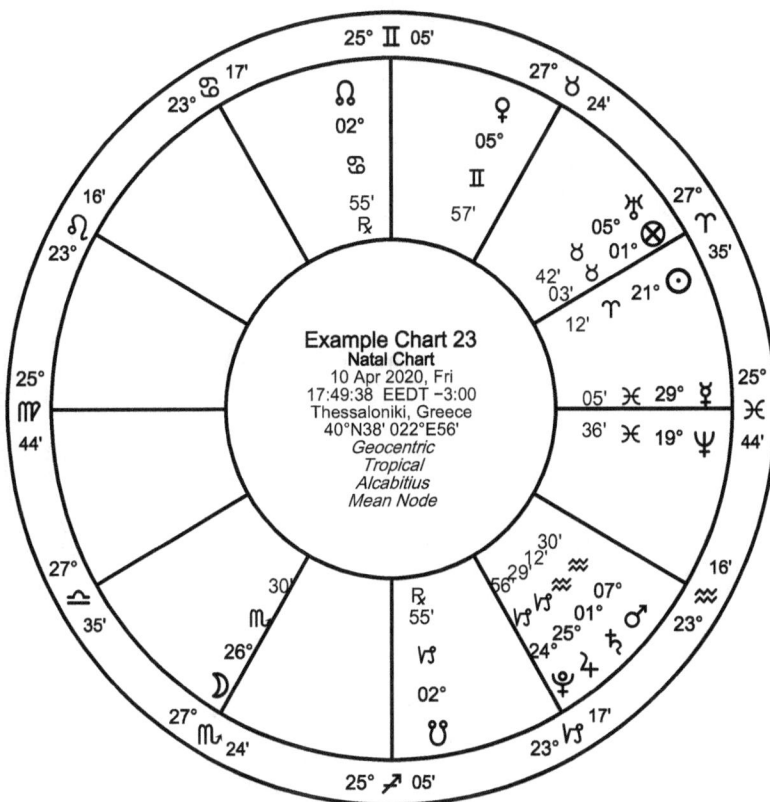

certainly NO. The conjunction was explained by the fact that they were about to go on a business trip together (they were colleagues).

Example Chart 23 was a 7th house question. The domicile ruler/almuten of the ascendant, Mercury, is in the 7th house, which makes him a 7th house significator as well. The Moon applies to a trine with Mercury and this is very positive. In fact, she is translating light from Jupiter, domicile ruler of the 7th house, to Mercury. Mercury is helped by his very strong mutual reception with Venus and Venus herself, almuten of the 7th house, applies to a trine with Mars, a fortunate next aspect. What more can one ask? The answer is a definite YES.

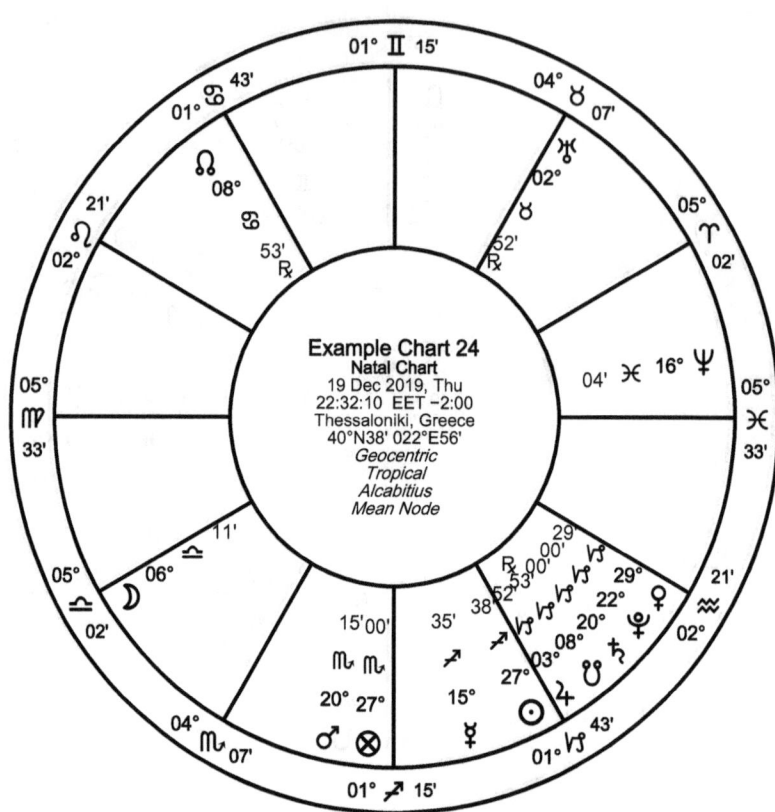

Example Chart 24 was a question about a misplaced item. We see the Moon in the 2nd house of possessions applying to a sextile with Mercury with reception (the Moon is in Mercury's triplicity and terms). This is good. Mercury has a mutual reception with Jupiter (domicile/terms) and he may be under the beams, but he won't be combust for quite some time, because the Sun is going to change signs before that happens. The Moon has a mutual reception with Saturn (exaltation/triplicity). All these are very fortunate testimonies and the item will be found. And so in fact it was.

Final Step – Chart Judgement

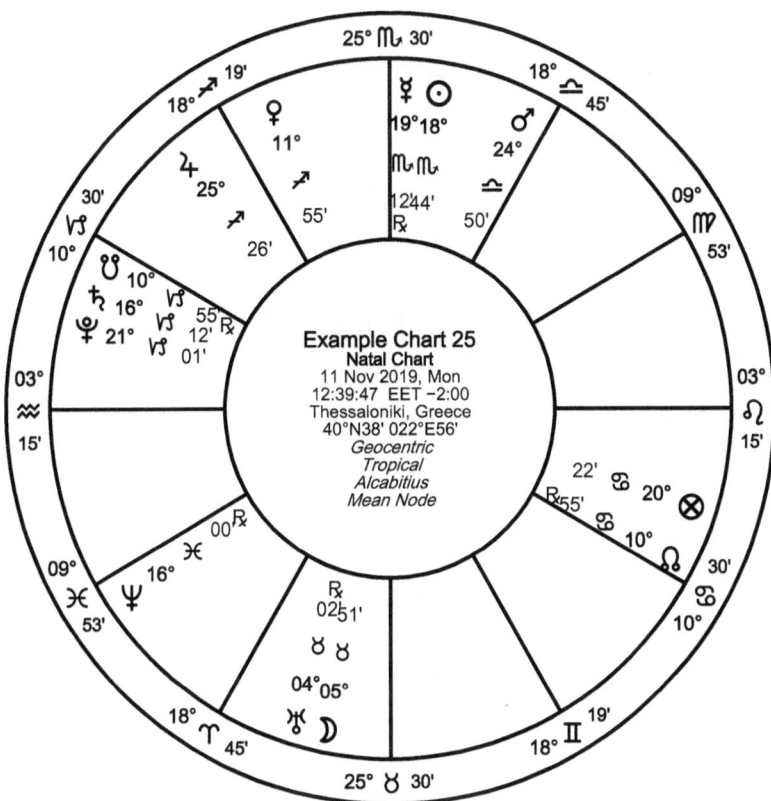

Example Chart 25 was another question about a misplaced item. The Moon is exalted and applies to a trine with Saturn in domicile. Saturn is the domicile ruler and almuten of the ascendant. Saturn rejoices in the 12th house and the conjunction with the South Node is not that debilitating, because he is also very strong essentially and he has a very strong mutual reception with Mars. The answer is YES.

We've reached the end of this book and I hope to have made chart judgement clearer. Naturally I haven't covered every possible astrological combination, but hopefully I have showed you a simple way to approach horary charts. To sum up, whatever the question is, evaluate the condition of the ruler(s) of the ascendant and the Moon and check what happens to them next (their applying aspects that is), the way I showed you in the chart examples. You will then do the same for the ruler of the quesited and in most cases, you will have a clear answer, provided you asked a valid question and the chart is radical. Remember: Don't play detective and don't write scripts at the expense of your client's money!

Appendix

Extra Charts for Further Practice

(Answers on p.96)

TRY FIRST TO APPLY the general rule without knowing what the question is. What are the next aspects of the main significators (domicile ruler/almuten of the ascendant and the Moon)? If they are fortunate (trines, sextiles with at least a single reception or between planets with lots of essential dignity, conjunctions with the Fortunes or with the Infortunes with strong receptions), then the answer is YES. If they are unfortunate (squares with the Infortunes and the Sun without a strong mutual reception, squares with the Fortunes in a bad state and without reception, all oppositions, unless there is a third planet in a sextile/trine relationship with the opposing planets that is receiving them, conjunctions with the Sun or the Infortunes without reception), then the answer is NO. See if and how often your answer changes once you find out what the quesited is.

Appendix: Extra Charts for Further Practice

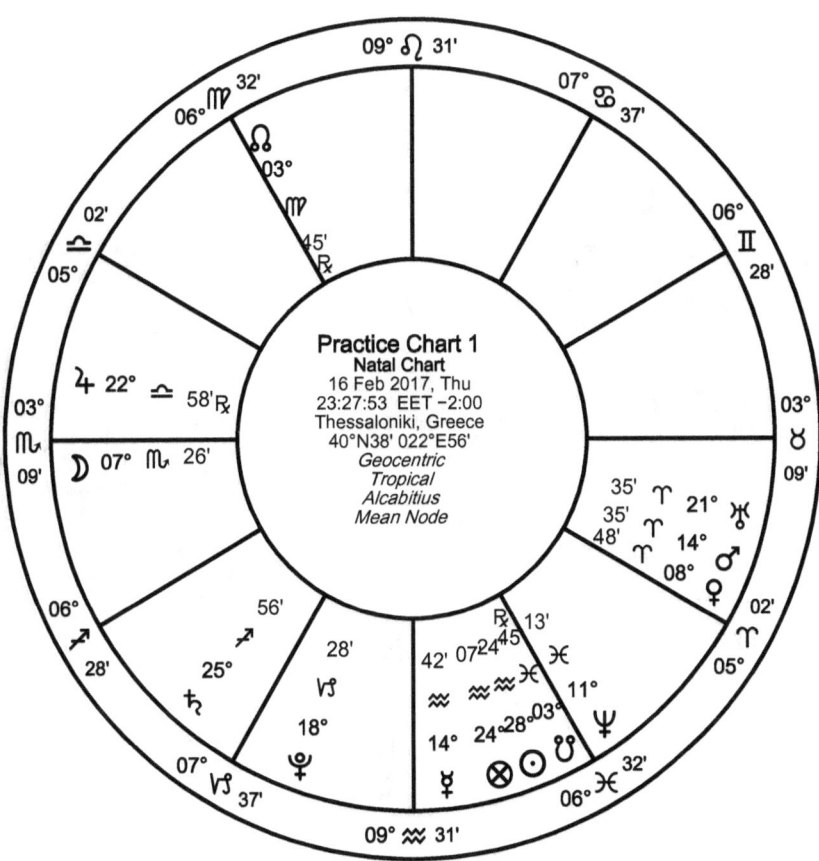

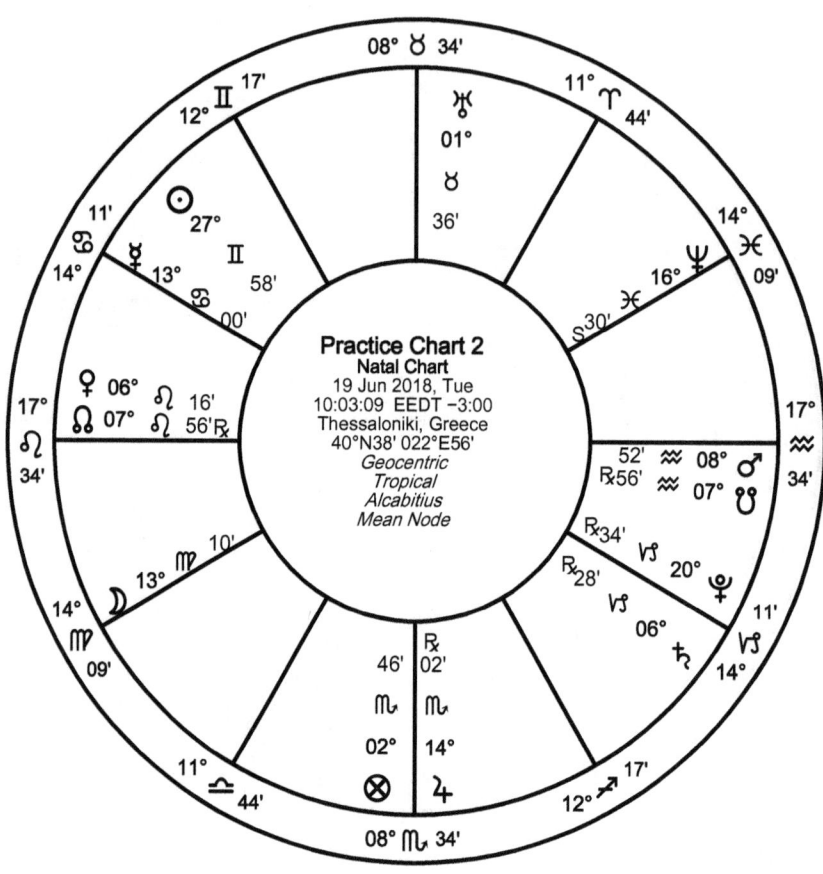

Appendix: Extra Charts for Further Practice 91

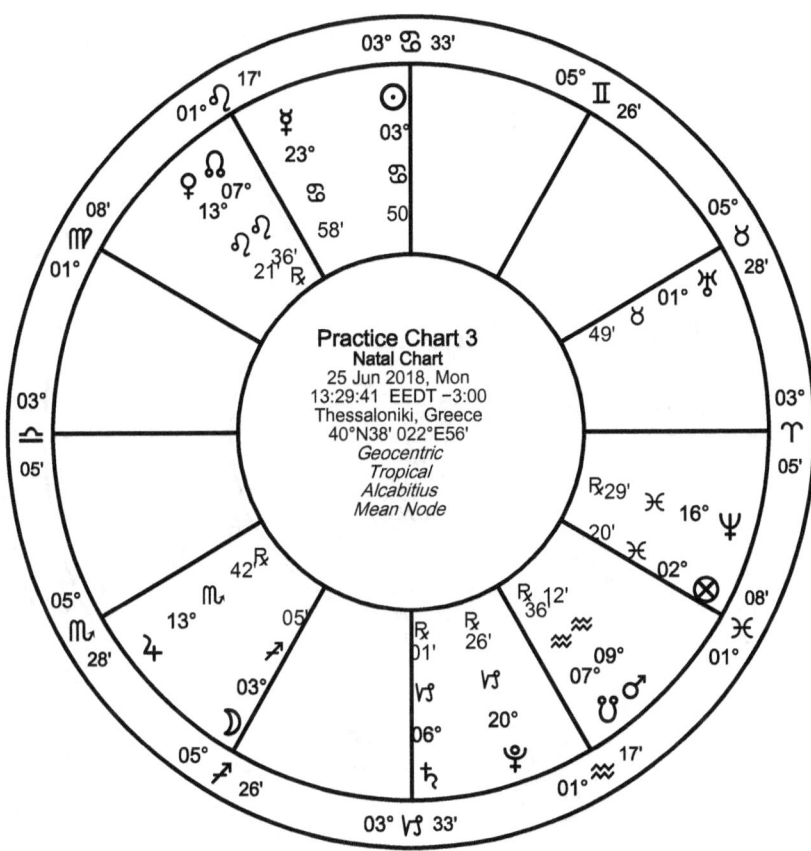

92 Horary Astrology Step by Step

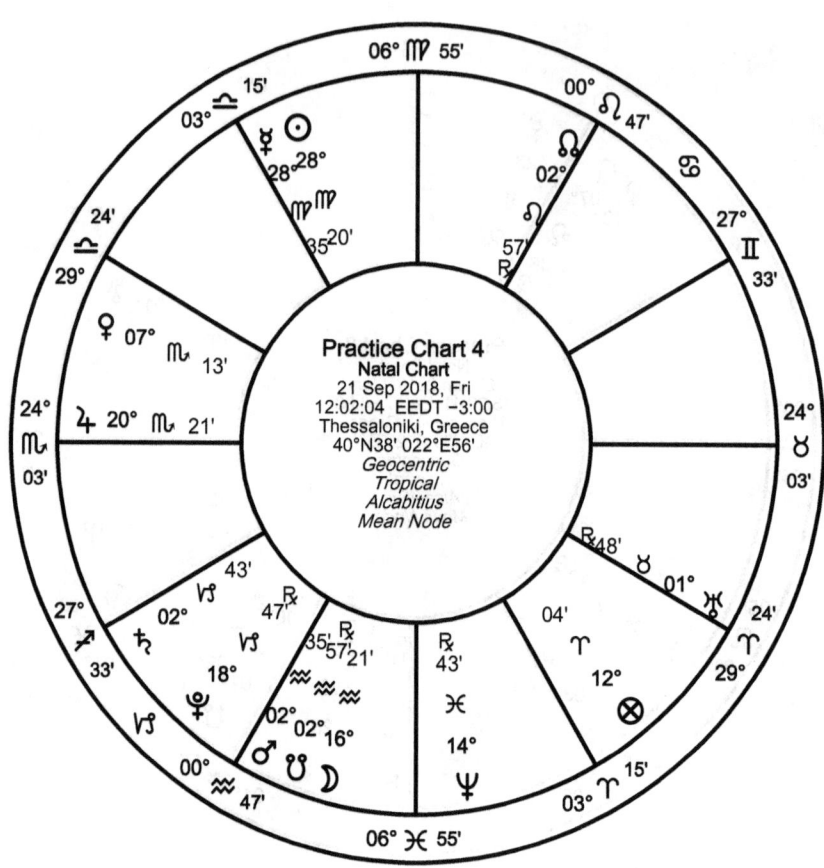

Appendix: Extra Charts for Further Practice

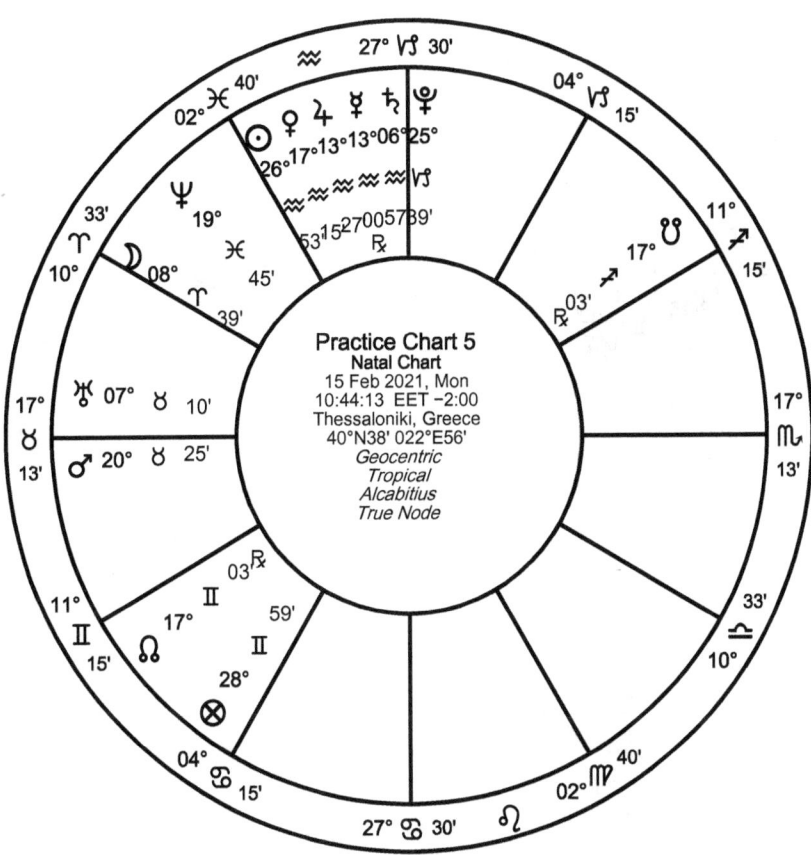

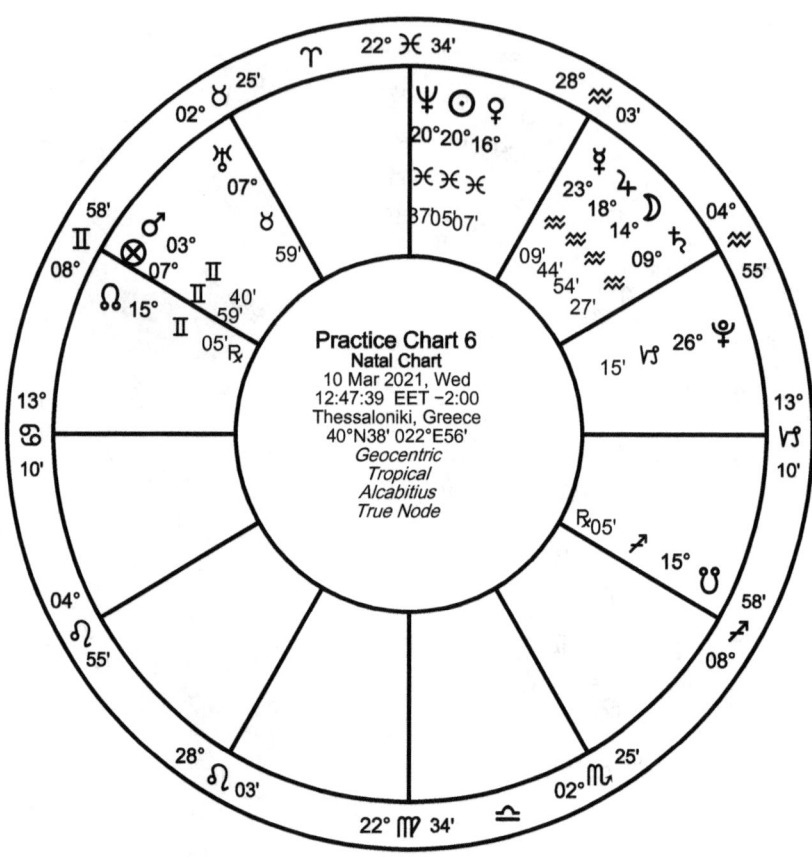

Appendix: Extra Charts for Further Practice 95

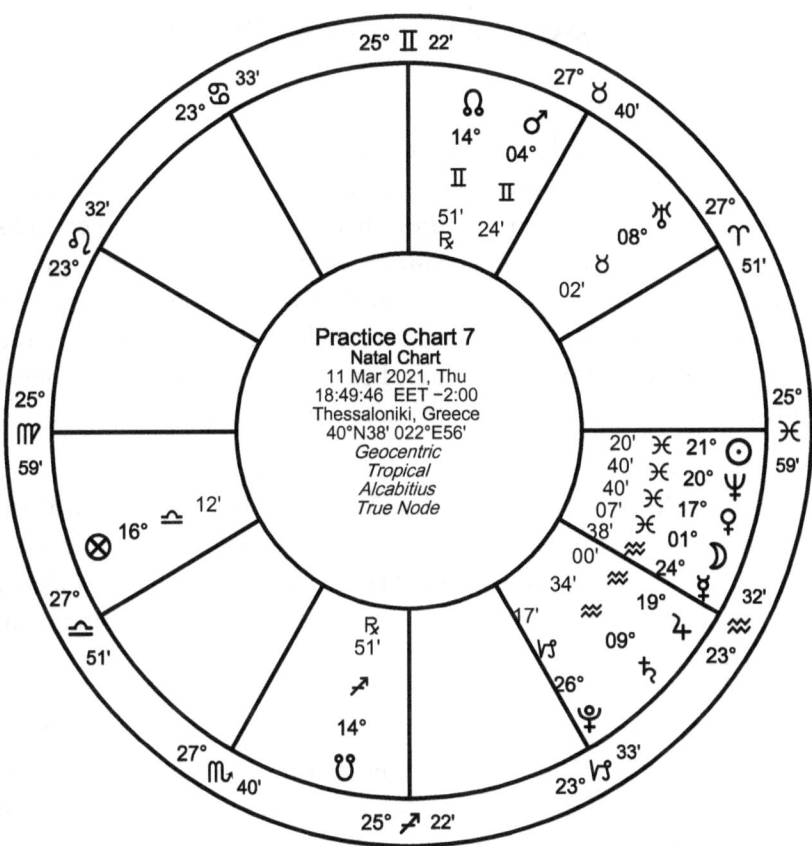

Answers to Practice Charts

Practice Chart 1

The Moon in fall applies to square Mercury without reception. Mars, domicile ruler and almuten of the ascendant is essentially strong in Aries, swift in motion and in the 6th house where he rejoices. His next aspect, however, is an opposition with retrograde Jupiter in the 12th house. Jupiter receives help from Saturn, but an opposition is an opposition. Even if we consider Saturn as able to reduce the harm of the Mars/Jupiter opposition, this cannot be called fortunate and combined with the Moon/Mercury square, the answer must be NO.

This is a sports question ("Will my team win?"). The Sun is the significator of the win. The Sun is in detriment and moving further away from Mars. The Moon will not make an aspect with the Sun for as long as she is in Scorpio and even if she did, it would be an ineffective square, hindered by the square with Mercury. The original negative answer is confirmed. The team lost the match.

Practice Chart 2

The Moon applies to a sextile with Jupiter, a Fortune. However, sextiles usually require at least a single reception for them to produce a positive outcome and there is no reception here. Besides that, Jupiter is retrograde. The Sun's (domicile and almuten of the ascendant) next aspect is a square with the Moon, although out of orb. Venus, co-significator of the querent since she is in the 1st house sign, applies to oppose Mars. The answer must be NO, but because of the Moon/Jupiter sextile, we need to become certain and the significators of the quesited must be checked.

This is a relationship question. Saturn, the domicile ruler and almuten of the 7th house, is in Capricorn, essentially strong but retrograde and cadent. Saturn makes no aspect with the Sun and the Moon is separating from him. Mars becomes a co-significator of the quesited and he forms an opposition with Venus. What's more, Mars in the 7th house is always a negative testimony in relationship questions. The answer is a definite NO. The relationship did not happen.

Practice Chart 3

Venus, domicile ruler of the ascendant, applies to square Jupiter. They are both Fortunes, but the reception is very weak, Jupiter is retrograde and he doesn't aspect the ascendant. The Moon applies to a sextile with Mars, but again, there is no reception between them and Mars is weakened by the conjunction with the South Node. So far, things are neither good nor particularly bad. Saturn, however, almuten of the ascendant, will soon oppose the Sun. That's very negative and the answer must be NO.

Another relationship question. The Sun is also the almuten of the 7th house and his opposition with Saturn is very serious. Venus is separating from an opposition with Mars. The Moon/Venus trine is hindered by the Venus/Jupiter square. They went out (the Moon/Mars sextile), but no relationship happened.

Practice Chart 4

Mars is the domicile ruler and almuten of the ascendant. He has a mutual reception with Saturn, but he is cadent and conjunct the South Node. His next aspect is a square with Venus (Venus is slowing down to turn retrograde and Mars is increasing in speed). A square without a mutual reception is a problem in most cases. Jupiter is conjunct the ascendant, which is good, because Jupiter is a Fortune. However, his next aspect is a square with the Moon without reception. The chart is not fortunate and whatever the question is, the answer must be NO.

It's a relationship question. Venus and Jupiter form squares with Mars and the Moon without strong receptions (the Moon is in the terms of Jupiter, but when the aspect perfects, she won't be). The relationship never happened.

Practice Chart 5

The Moon is in Aries, applying with a sextile to all the planets in Aquarius except Saturn. This is quite good, despite the fact that the Moon is in the 12th house. Her first aspect is a sextile with Mercury and there is reception (she will be in Mercury's terms when the aspect becomes exact). The ascendant domicile ruler and almuten is Venus, who is one of the planets in Aquarius. They are all helped a lot by

Saturn's presence there, who receives them. Venus is under the beams and close to combustion, but before that happens, the Sun will move into Pisces and there can be no combustion with the Sun in a different sign from the planet in question. Venus' next aspect is a sextile with the Moon. Mars is in detriment in the ascendant, but he is greatly helped by the mutual reception with the Moon. Not a terribly fortunate chart, but the amswer must be YES.

It's a job question. All the planets in Aquarius are co-significators of the job and the Moon sextiles them. Mars is the almuten of the 10th house and the fact that he is in the house of the querent is very positive, but if the mutual reception with the Moon weren't there, the result would have probably been different because Mars is an Infortune in detriment.

Practice Chart 6
The Moon, also domicile ruler and almuten of the ascendant, applies to conjunct Jupiter, a Fortune, and Saturn receives them both in his own sign. No need to look any further. The answer is YES. The only problem is the 8th house where the two planets are located and there might be difficulties along the way.

A question about sport. Jupiter, the 10th house domicile ruler, becomes a main significator. The Sun and Venus, a Fortune, are conjunct the MC (the win). Venus is not destroyed by the combustion, because she is exalted. Mars, domicile ruler of the intercepted sign in the 10th house, is applying with a trine to Saturn and Saturn receives him in his triplicity. Mars is in the 12th house, though. The querent's team won, but it wasn't easy.

Practice Chart 7
The Moon is received by exalted Venus, but she applies to Mars with a square. Mars receives the Moon in his triplicity, but he is an Infortune and the aspect is a square, so a strong mutual reception is needed. Mercury is the domicile ruler and almuten of the ascendant and he is received by Saturn in his own sign. He is in the unfortunate 6th house, though. The square between the Moon and Mars says it all. Whatever the question might be, the answer must be NO.

Appendix: Extra Charts for Further Practice

A job question. Mercury is also the 10th house ruler and makes no applying aspect in the sign he is in. The Moon/Mars square without a strong mutual reception leaves little doubt about the outcome. The querent didn't get the job.

Qualifying Horary Practitioner

Certificate and Diploma

Established 1984

The Qualifying Horary Practitioner (QHP) is a correspondence course divided into a Certificate and a Diploma. For the Diploma course, students can choose one of two modules: Horary or Nativities & Horary. By the end of the Diploma course, students are expected to make an accurate, verifiable prediction from an Interrogation (horary chart). This, together with continual assessment, replaces a final examination. After demonstrating that the lessons have reached a professional standard, students are awarded the Diploma. The QHP Diploma entitles the holder to use the initials QHP (Qualifying Horary Practitioner).

The QHP also offers a unique and brand new module: QHP *Nativities & Horary*. Certainly the most important of all charts, the pre-eminence of the Nativity is confirmed by William Lilly (1602-1681) and his contemporaries. No promising Horary can contradict the testimony of the Nativity. Alongside the more general testimony of the Nativity, the more precise testimony of the Horary reveals information relating to a specific enquiry at a specific point in time. In deploying the testimony of the Nativity alongside the Horary (and other charts), the practitioner is able to provide a more complete analysis and interpretation. It is for this purpose that the QHP offers a unique new course, combining both horary and genethliacal (natal) techniques, devised by QHP Head Tutor, Petros Eleftheriadis.

Both the existing QHP Diploma Module (*Horary*) and the new QHP Diploma Module (*Nativities & Horary*) are designed primarily for QHP Certificate holders. The QHP Certificate is a one year course divided into six lessons covering the basic techniques relating to Interrogational (Horary) astrology. Certificate holders from other courses and other interested students are also welcome, provided that the required level of competence in astrological theory can be demonstrated. The new QHP Module is particularly concerned with predictive techniques applied to Nativities, such as primary directions, secondary progressions, solar and lunar returns, profections and so on. Yet, this new module also builds upon the theory and practice of horary techniques taught at QHP Certificate level in its application of these techniques to a wider range of charts. Successful completion of this new QHP Module entitles the holder to the initials QHP (Qualifying Horary Practitioner).

For more information, visit the QHP site (https://qhpastrology.co.uk) or contact me at: petelefth@gmail.com

www.ingramcontent.com/pod-product-compliance
Lightning Source LLC
Chambersburg PA
CBHW071008160426
43193CB00012B/1972